Introduction

I grew up with the Beatles, not in the sense that they lived around the corner from me and were my classmates in school. No, they grew up in the concert halls, stadiums, and studios of the world, while I, living in a suburb of Kansas City, followed the more prescribed route of junior high, high school, and finally college on the West Coast.

But the Beatles and I were friends nonetheless. This book is the story of that friendship.

It's a highly personal story, but it tells of the one thing we all held in common during the violent, uncertain Sixties. Personal, yes, but perhaps the reader, in hearing the echoes of the screams of Beatlemania, will conjure up the images of his own life at that time. Perhaps he will dust off his partly forgotten collection of Beatle records and play them once again, to recapture the joys and the sadness of the past years.

It is my hope that the reader will discover himself—or herself—in these pages. It's everyone's story as well as mine.

The Beatles, as one musicologist put it, have passed into our collective subconscious. They are a cultural yardstick by which other popular music is measured and, all too often, found lacking. Each Beatles album set new standards of excellence in arrangement, production, and artistry. Their lyrics, sometimes soaring to the level of poetry, at other times piercing the depths of personal pain, are written in the language of youth, energy, and experience.

The Beatles created a world, with themselves as its leaders and with us as their willing subjects.

Growing Up with the Beatles is chronological in structure, covering the years 1964 to 1976, but the story does not follow a strict sequence of time. I heard about the group when they first became popular in America but did not consider myself a "fan" until three years later. Only then did I begin exploring the Beatles' history, from Liverpool to Hamburg to London and the world, and taking an interest in their personalities as well as the makeup of their music. The book follows *my* year-by-year experience with the group, which was not necessarily the way anyone else might have encountered them. Also, as a school child, I always felt that a year really began and ended in September; consequently, the chapters seldom break off neatly on New Year's Eve. My "years" were usually determined by personal events, not by the calendar.

The Beatles appeared, as if by magic, at every important juncture of my life. Their music was played at the parties where I discovered the embarrassment and the thrill of asking a girl to dance. The Beatles appeared like smiling, encouraging companions on the cinema screen as I fumbled my way through my first date. Their songs welled up in moments of pain and loneliness, as if to say, "We know. We understand. We're here." At the time they split up, I too broke away from my family, my friends, the places I had known all my life, to attend school in California. As I drove over the hills into the Los Angeles basin, a new song by John Lennon crackled on the car radio, as if the Beatles were saying, "We're with you. You haven't left us behind."

The Beatles are like a habit I can't shake. I still anticipate the release of their solo albums, and save all the news articles about them that appear in the papers. I can't hear their music now without encountering the same emotions and images I experienced in the past. When I need to relate to, say, 1967, instead of thinking of political or personal events, I realize it was the year that *Sgt. Pepper* came out, and everything falls into place.

John Lennon sang that the dream was over. Not completely, John; we have our memories. The remembered taste of honey will always be sweeter than the current taste of salt.

Thank you, Beatles, for being with me when I was growing up.

Ron Schaumburg
Kansas City
June 1976

To the Fab Four
John, Paul, George, and Ringo
with thanks and love

Growing Up With THE BEATLES

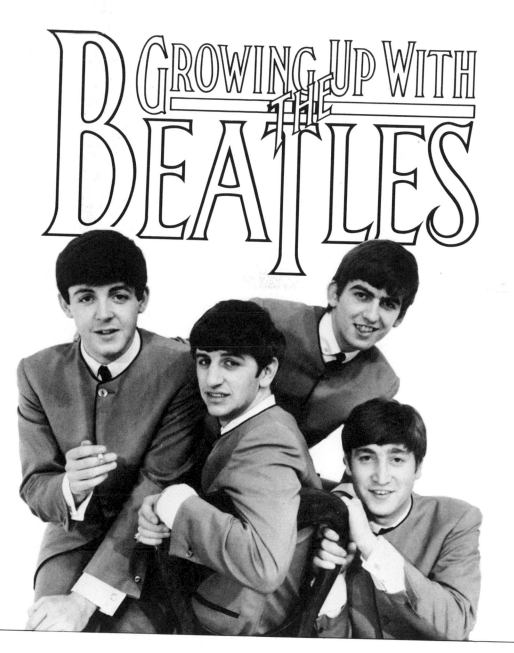

An illustrated tribute by Ron Schaumburg

PYRAMID BOOKS ▲ NEW YORK

Contents

Great to have you with us

George Harrison

Ringo Starr

Paul McCartney

John Lennon

1964

*. . . when love was a matter of holding hands
and "yeah, yeah, yeah!" meant she loved you
and we were glad
and we were new . . .*

I can remember the very first time I heard the Beatles. It was in a drug store in Roeland Park, Kansas, on a cold afternoon in late January. I was eleven years old, skinny (but wiry), big-eared and be-spectacled. On the sixth-grade football field I was as useless as feathers on a frog, but at schoolwork I was an academic Michelangelo.

My family lived on a tree-lined street in a white two-story house with a front yard, and a vegetable garden and a swing set in back. There were three children. I had to share a room with my brother Robert, seven years old, while Susie, thirteen, had a room all to herself. Our pet dog, Cozy, the poorest excuse for a pedigreed poodle I've ever seen, spent her nights snoozing happily in an unused bathtub in the basement. My room was decorated with cowboy wallpaper. On the shelves were the countless souvenir corncob pipes, statuettes, and seashells I had hauled back from the trips to the Ozarks, Colorado, San Francisco, and the Eastern Seaboard.

Being eleven years old put me in a very awkward spot. I wasn't old enough to be a "big kid" and stay up till all hours (ten thirty at least!), but I was too big to enjoy stuffed animals and cowboys-and-Indians. My hair was cropped to a barely adequate furry fringe. My ears were thus exposed to the world, and the glasses I started wearing a year earlier made them stick out much more than I thought was necessary. Fortunately the braces I wore in fourth grade had eliminated my front-tooth gap and my overbite, so I didn't look *too* much like a gopher with goggles. As if my Don Knotts-like appearance wasn't enough, I was probably the smartest boy in my class. *That* is enough to lose you friends for life.

"Oh, you don't have to study," other kids would say before a big test. "You always get A's." How did they think I got them? Gift-wrapped at Christmas?

I read like a monk, and my parents indulged my habit. From book clubs came such treasures as *Dickens' Christmas Stories, The Adventures of Huckleberry Finn*, and *Swiss Family Robinson. American Heritage* provided histories of Indians, whaling ships, and railroading. We still had the books my mother had read as a child, like *Winnie-the-Pooh*. My favorites were E. Nesbit's Bastable Children stories, from which Mom read aloud to us each night. I read *Alice in Wonderland* and Dr. Seuss books with delight. Each summer I checked out two books a week from my school library. I always got through the school reading programs faster than some of the other kids, so I had more time to read "my" books.

At home after school my time was divided between television, homework, and practicing piano. My best friend Ricky Patrick and I watched the Mickey Mouse Club reruns religiously while snarfing Oreos and potato chips. I had to practice piano a half hour

The Schaumburg Clan, Juvenile Division: Robert on the left, Susie on the right, and me. The height of fashion for early 1964.

7

a day. Those Kuhlau sonatinas and Czerny finger exercises we had to play were as monotonous as a metronome. The John Thompson books offered a little

(Above) Anyone could wear the national fan-club button, but only Kansas Citians could join radio station WHB's local chapter. My sister faithfully enlisted; I observed from the sidelines. (Below and opposite) The Beatles, in their natty trend-setting clothes, cavort for photographers.

more melodic variety, but I felt insulted that I was still playing in the fourth-grade book even though I was two years beyond that in school. I loved playing Thompson's simplified versions of themes from Beethoven's Fifth Symphony and Massenet's "Melodie." More than once, though, I slammed the keyboard with my fist out of frustration and anger at being incapable of playing complex passages. All three of us Schaumburg children took lessons. Our teacher was an old Italian maestro named Mr. Rendina.

"Too many bum notes!" he would yell, slapping our hands—hard. He could hurt, too. Our half-hour lessons often either stretched into hour-long tortures or ended fifteen minutes early with Mr. Rendina stalking out in anger.

Susie, at thirteen, was practicing to be a teenager, experimenting with makeup and hair styles and trying to take more pride in her appearance. Dad had given her a record player. I listened to the few singles she bought, like "It's My Party" and "Judy's Turn to Cry," "Telstar," "Butterfly Baby," "Living Right Next Door to an Angel," "Patches," "Dominique," "Tammy," "Blue Velvet," "Bobby's Girl," and a number of Beach Boy records. I had a transistor radio that I'd won by selling Christmas cards door-to-door. It had a speaker about the size of a Necco wafer and an earphone that felt like a pencil jabbed into my ear when I listened under the covers at night.

My parents owned a few records, mostly boxed sets of classics. They gave us a few children's records, including one which told a tale about a little bullfighter. While it played, we acted out the story, running around through the house, leaping into the air at every crescendo. My father composed a piano piece which produced the same effect. I called it the "Skipping Song." I loved hearing the yellow plastic Golden Records which mostly featured Disney songs. I liked the "Siamese Cat Song," from *Lady and the*

(Top) Beatlemania at its most commercial; there were also guitars, drums, notebooks, even tennis shoes, all bearing the Beatle name. (Above) The Beatles wonder open-mouthed at their success. (Opposite) Cards, buttons, bracelets, and magazines reveal the impact of the Fab Four on the U.S.

Tramp, although I had no idea what it was about.

I had, I suppose, somewhat unusual interests for my age. In second grade I wanted to be a farmer, because I loved carrots and wanted to grow them. Because of my carrot mania and the fact that my nose twitches when I blink my eyes, my mother started calling me "Rabbit." As I reached the fourth grade, though, I thought I'd like to become a writer and started composing poems, plays, and a short story or two. While the other guys could spot makes and models of cars from a hundred paces, I couldn't tell a Volkswagen from a Volvo. To this day I can't say for certain if the Kansas City Royals are in the American League or the National League. When it came to building model cars, I was an expert at putting wheels where the windshield belonged and at getting gluey fingerprints all over the car's body and mine.

But the things I *did* know and like, I loved passionately. Many a happy Saturday afternoon was spent with Ricky and my neighbor Kevin White as we traipsed along a nearby creek hunting for fossils like little Lewis Leakeys. I blew a week's allowance on a book called *Fossils: A Guide to Prehistoric Life.* I stuffed it in my knapsack along with a hammer, chisel, and sack lunch, and spent the day getting muddy and chopping away loose Kansas sedimentary rock, returning with a precious handful of crinoid stems and bivalve mollusks. I always secretly hoped to find a dinosaur bone but had to be content with writing a poem about discovering a Brontosaurus, alive and well, buried up to his neck along the creek.

Abraham Lincoln was another passion. I collected articles, photographs, and books about him. I ran a "Lincoln Museum" in the playroom, which consisted of plastic statues and memorabilia I'd amassed while in Washington. The museum lived only a very short time.

Every year I celebrated Lincoln's birthday by

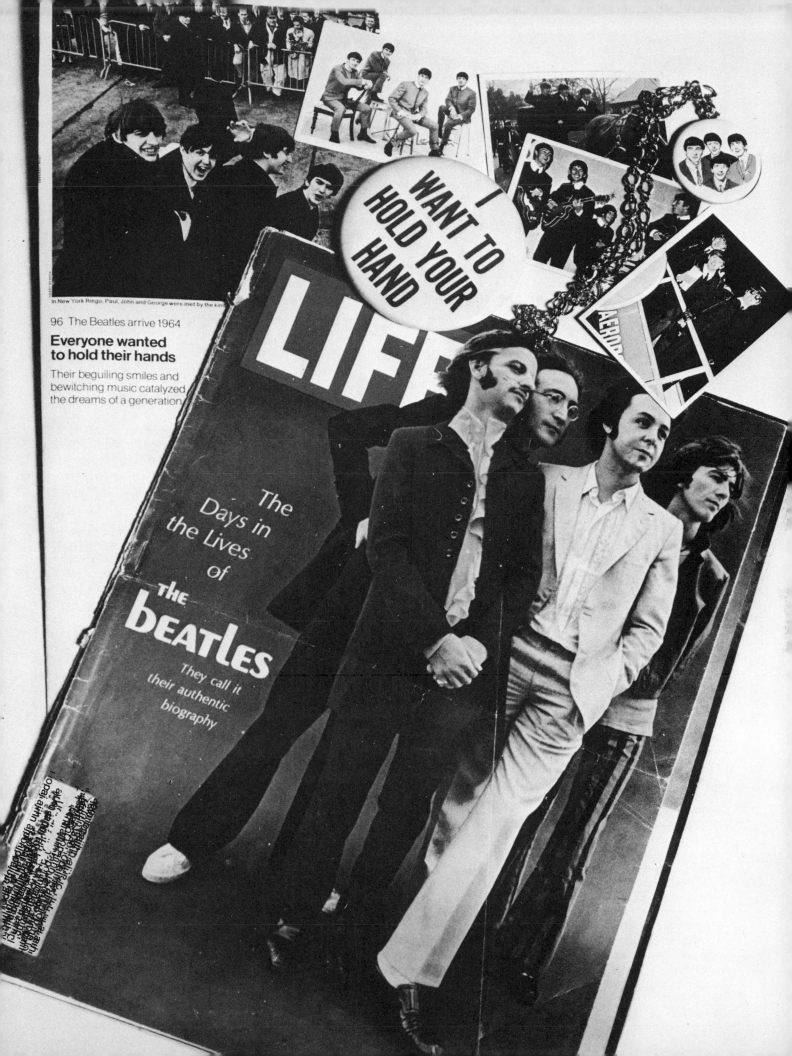

96 The Beatles arrive 1964

**Everyone wanted
to hold their hands**

Their beguiling smiles and
bewitching music catalyzed
the dreams of a generation.

In New York Ringo, Paul, John and George were met by the kind

I WANT TO HOLD YOUR HAND

LIFE

The
Days in
the Lives
of

THE
beatles

They call it
their authentic
biography

throwing a little party for him in the basement. I got so excited about it that I bought the party treats and candy weeks in advance. That's why I was in the drug store the day I heard the Beatles. As I walked through the aisles clutching my bags of Valentine's hearts, I heard the scratchy sound of the hi-fi department's two-speed record player. Despite the distortion of high volume, the music was unlike any I'd heard before.

"What's that song?" I asked the salesclerk. "It's kinda neat."

"It's by a new group called the Beatles," she said. " 'I Want to Hold Your Hand.' "

You're not holding mine, I thought, and left.

During recess the next day, a group of us stood under the dark, cold clouds of a Kansas winter. Some of the fellows were off playing kickball, but since I was usually the last one chosen, I didn't feel needed or welcome there. My teacher once tried to coach me privately in the fine art of football tossing, but little of it rubbed off. I usually hung around the jungle gym, taking as little part as possible in competitive sports. Just to make conversation I said to the others hanging by their heels, "Hey, have you guys heard that new song by . . . uh . . . by . . . ." I stopped cold. I couldn't remember the title, or the name of the group, or one note of the melody, so no one had any idea what I was talking about. It was to be the last time I'd ever forget the Beatles' name.

My world was a small one in those days, seen mostly through the eye of a television set. At eleven, my personal history was short: I remember running to school as quickly as I could on the morning of February 20, 1962, to watch John Glenn's blast-off on the school TV and to pray that it all went smoothly. Bad dreams haunted me after I saw TV advertisements showing what action to take in case of fallout from nuclear attack. In one dream I was trying to reach the safety of our basement after an attack, but I grew dizzy and sick and started to disintegrate before the horrified eyes of my family. I was aware of the racial tension of the South, although it was not very visible in my all-white community. I understood that Kennedy had been killed two months before, but it meant little to me, other than the fact that television shows were canceled for five straight days. My world was cozy and sheltered, and did not extend far beyond the Neosho Lane neighborhood.

The wave of Beatlemania, however, was about to break. It had swamped England in 1963, leaving screaming teenagers and amused, bemused parents in its wake. Even the royal family took a casual interest in the shaggy quartet. It's still hard to believe that in January 1964 America didn't know who the Beatles were, but that two weeks later we were talking of nothing else.

Shortly before the Beatles arrived in the United States on February 7, 1964, I became aware of the vast excitement that surrounded them. "I Want to Hold Your Hand" had reached the number-one spot in America, and the local dime stores were suddenly flooded with Beatle wigs, buttons, shirts, dolls, rings, lunchboxes, notebooks, and tennis shoes. Baskin-Robbins even introduced "Beatle Nut" ice cream. A col-

(Above) The first glimpse most Americans had of the Beatles was on the Ed Sullivan Show. (Opposite bottom) Road manager Mal Evans helps Ringo set up while Ed coaches a stand-in for the flu-stricken George. (Opposite top) George, looking a bit out of it, made it for the broadcast.

umnist in a Kansas City paper pointed out that the last time beetles came to the country we ignored them, and look what happened to the elm trees. Eleven years later, in 1975, *Life* magazine, in a publication called *The 100 Events That Shaped America,* listed the Beatles' arrival in position 96.

I remember how the Beatles' appearances on the *Ed Sullivan Show* on February 9 and 16, 1964, set the schoolyard buzzing with anticipation. Like 73,000,000 other Americans my friends and I sat in front of our television sets, watching as the Beatles sang through such songs as "She Loves You," "All My Loving," "I Saw Her Standing There," and "Twist and Shout." A friend of mine, Kathy Atkinson, says her father made her watch because it would be something she'd "always want to remember." "I hated it," she recalls. "At that time I hated anything my father *made* me do."

I watched, partly because of the general interest in the Beatles, but mainly because Ed Sullivan, like *Bonanza* and *My Favorite Martian,* was part of my regular Sunday night routine. My homework was usually done by the time Sunday night rolled around, so there was time for fun. Besides, the chief topic of conversation during any school day was the previous night's TV shows, and I didn't want to feel out of place or uninformed.

Television was the ideal medium for introducing the Beatles. Jack Paar, in fact, thought so too, and had actually presented the first videotape of the group in America on his January 3 program. So although the Ed Sullivan shows were not the first time

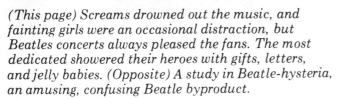

(This page) Screams drowned out the music, and fainting girls were an occasional distraction, but Beatles concerts always pleased the fans. The most dedicated showered their heroes with gifts, letters, and jelly babies. (Opposite) A study in Beatle-hysteria, an amusing, confusing Beatle byproduct.

the Beatles graced the airwaves, it was the first time I and millions of others had seen them. Television offered the sound of a radio, the movement of film, and the immediacy of a newspaper, and sent it all, free of charge, into American living rooms. During Sullivan's show we could see the Beatles singing and shaking those wild haircuts. Hysterical girls screamed out, "John!" "I love you, Paul!" "Auugghh!" "Look at me, George!" "RINGO!!" on live TV. I had never seen anything like it before. I thought they must have paid the audience, or at least rehearsed them. As the camera panned from one Beatle to another, their names were flashed on the screen. Under John's name appeared the parenthetical admonition "Sorry, girls, he's married." Stoneface Ed *did* have a sense of

humor after all.

I was thrilled. When the Beatles came on I left my seat to get closer to the screen, much as armchair quarterbacks do during the instant replay of a touchdown. I was as amazed by the Beatles as I was by the audience reaction to them. Why, why, *why* were girls behaving that way? "Look at them!" I said to no one in particular, "they're going crazy!"

While we kids thrilled, so too did our parents. The Beatles, with their revolutionary haircuts (though they are obviously conservative by today's standards) and their charming mannerisms, seemed "clean" to most teenagers' mothers, an image which the Beatles were later to satirize in *A Hard Day's Night.* The Beatles' clothes also set them apart. At the time, my

own wardrobe consisted of dorky print shirts, baggy trousers, and scuffed black penny loafers. I hated to tie shoes. My hair was as short and fuzzy as lint from a clothes dryer. Sunday dress-up found me in a white shirt with a too-tight collar, a brown tweed suit coat, scratchy brown pants, and the same scuffed black penny loafers. I alternated between bow-ties and skinny black neckties, both of which clipped on at the neck. I realized later that Brian Epstein had been shrewd in polishing his boys' image, dressing them in spiffy collarless gray suits, pointed black boots, and shaggy haircuts.

I found that most parents of my friends accepted, if not openly endorsed, the Beatles, in sharp preference to "those greasy rock-and-rollers" or "that noisy *garbage*" that poured from radios. Some adults even enjoyed their music. A seventy-eight-year-old man said to me, "Yeah, I like the Beatles. Watch them on television. They's pretty good, ain't they?" Some mothers seemed amused, because they remembered their Sinatras and Presleys. Yet political and religious figures, like Khrushchev and Billy Graham, denounced the group as "a corrupting influence meant to distract youthful minds from politics" or as "a passing fad." To me the Beatles were neither. They were fun. They were exciting. And they played good music.

The girls at school started going collectively crazy. In the weeks that followed the Sullivan shows, they exchanged the treasured nickels of their allowances for the infinite variety of Beatle artifacts. Bubble gum trading cards began to circulate, and even the boys who couldn't stand the group started to let their hair grow. My father finally gave up trying to make my hair stand on end and retired our jar of Butch Wax. I know of more than one fellow who pocketed his haircut money instead of going to the barber shop. Some of the kids tried to imitate the Beatle accent, although few had even heard of Liverpool before. Others wanted the Cuban boots and collarless jackets the group wore. I never actually saw the clothes in stores or knew anyone who owned them.

I somehow felt that guys weren't really supposed to

(Opposite) John in a casual moment with wife Cynthia during the first U.S. tour. (Below left) The Gang: a Beatle-shaggy Ricky Patrick and I flank our buddies from school. (Above) A cruelly retouched bubble gum card and a deceiving shot of Lennon which touched off a small schoolyard panic.

like the Beatles, but their music so transcended anything else on the radio that I couldn't help falling under their spell. As if a little war were raging, I entrenched myself in no-man's-land, tactfully playing both sides of the conflict. I listened in as the girls talked their Beatle talk and sang their Beatle song:

> We love you, Beatles
> Oh yes we do
> We don't love anyone
> Better than you
> When you're not with us
> We're blue
> Oh Be-ea-tles, we love you!

But I could also jeer along with the fellows as they lobbed sneering insults into the girls' territory. It seems like such nonsense now, but it was life and death back then.

One day a girl named Agnes, one of the more vociferous Beatle fans, came out at recess and was unusually quiet.

"What's wrong?" someone asked, noticing her look of pain.

With a sob Agnes wiped a tear from her eye and pulled a bubble gum card from her pocket. "He's hurt!" she cried.

"What?" the girls gasped, crowding around the card. It was a picture of John Lennon, photographed at such an angle that he appeared to have only four fingers on his right hand.

Agnes burst into a fresh flood of tears. The girls tried to console her.

"It's all right, Agnes, it's *only* a picture."

"It's just the camera angle, don't worry."

"He couldn't *play* if he only had four fingers!"

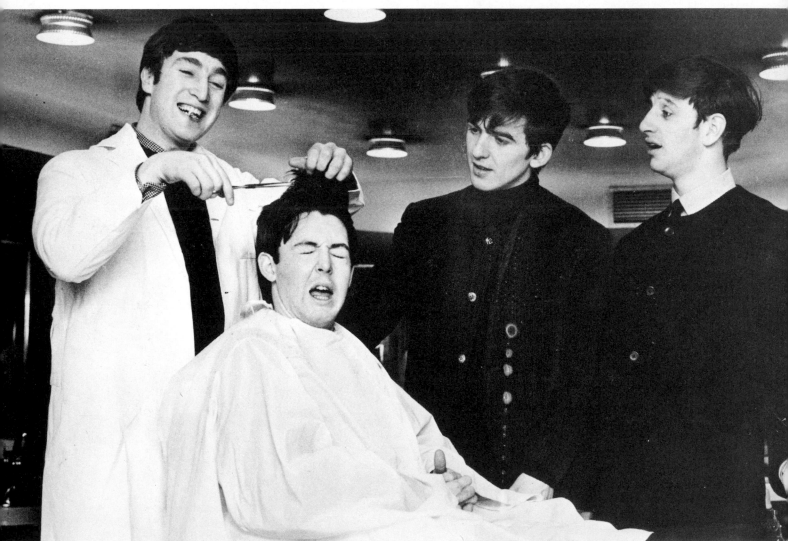

But no amount of consoling or explaining would convince Agnes that her idol was still whole; she was convinced Lennon's tragic secret was out.

A friend of mine, Mary Lee Wilson, "played pretend," and imagined she and her friends were Beatle wives. "At first," she remembers, "we had fist fights over who would marry Paul, but we couldn't have cared less about John." Later, however, they pretended to "kill Cynthia Lennon off in a car wreck so that John would be lonely." The girls then stuffed their brassieres with paper and "appeared" in front of Lennon to comfort him. As Beatle wives they talked as if their husbands were away doing a concert somewhere. If there were too many girls at a slumber party, some pretended to be the Beatles themselves, and the others gave them "haircuts." They fantasized that they had children. Sometimes they concocted bizarre tragedies to dramatize, like having John's son cling to life desperately after having swallowed a pin.

While the girls were indulging their dreams, I was enacting my own as a "Basement Beatle." Ricky and I took my sister's record player downstairs. With Kevin joining us, we banged away on my mother's flour canisters and twanged away on invisible guitars, mouthing the words to "She Loves You," "I Want to Hold Your Hand," "All My Loving," "Please Please Me," "Love Me Do," and "I Wanna Be Your Man." We performed without an audience, but we took great care to be accurate. Ricky, who took after Lennon, had mastered John's cocky, sexy, spread-legged stance; Kevin had Paul's left-handed style down pat, and as I had no preference for any single Beatle, I was content to struggle along with Ringo's beat. My brother Robert had formed a similar group, but they were a little more imaginative. They used tennis rackets as guitars, and wore Beatle wigs when they performed for the second-grade music class. Our "Basement Beatles" soon broke up, however. My mother confiscated the flour canisters when she saw the dents I'd put in them with the spoons I used for drumsticks.

One night my father surprised me—he came home with copies of the first official Beatles posters. The photograph was one in which Ringo sits on a chair with the others grouped around him. Paul, John, and George each have one foot placed awkwardly on the chair. George stands between John and Paul, his hands on their shoulders, looking slightly away from the camera. Paul holds a cigarette in his left hand, and they are all dressed in matching gray collarless suits with black trimming and the standard black boots. The distinctive "Beatles" logo stands in the lower right-hand corner. I was surprised that even my father was aware of how important the group was. He occasionally brought home penny candy but never anything like this! The posters cost fifty cents at the time, but I wouldn't part with mine now for an autographed sequin from an Elton John concert. The poster still hangs on a wall in my room.

Meanwhile the Beatles, unconcerned with the hoopla around them, were recording the best music of the decade. *Meet the Beatles* was their first major American release, and it came out on January 20,

1964. I later found out that the English version of this album, called *With the Beatles*, was released on November 22, 1963, the same day President Kennedy was assassinated. As one youthful leader died, the young looked for another to take his place, and the Beatles appeared. With such songs as "She Loves You," "I Saw Her Standing There," "All My Loving," "I'll Get You," "Can't Buy Me Love," "And I Love Her," and "This Boy," Lennon and McCartney began to be compared with Shubert and Beethoven. All the record companies that had rights to the early recordings began re-releasing them to cash in on the group's swelling popularity. The songs I call the "terrible twelve"—"Anna," "Boys," and "Chains," for example—were repackaged half-a-dozen ways. Record company people began to realize that the Beatles meant business. Young fans began to realize that they could be too easily swindled, if they didn't examine records closely enough to discover they were the same ones that had appeared a month before with a different cover.

(Opposite) America greets the Fab Four with painted windows and a flood of novelties from a Woolworth's display table, while the Beatles oblige photographers in a barber shop. (Below) One of Dezo Hoffman's beautiful portraits, from which series came the first official U.S. Beatles poster.

John Lennon made me jealous in March by publishing a short collection of his nonsense verse and drawings called *In His Own Write*. I had visions of greatness myself and had wanted to publish my own stories. In fact, Ricky, Kevin, and I had even set up a small publishing firm with the unwieldy name of *Ron Schaumburg Kevin White Rick Patrick Books Cards and What-Not Printers and Publishers*. We had collaborated on a tacky handmade calendar the year before, and tried to sell it around the neighborhood. One man gave us fifty cents out of pity, and my mother finally informed us that "insurance companies give out nicer ones for free." *Sic transit* calendars. We turned our efforts to mass-producing the stories and poems I wrote, specifically the dinosaur one, producing it as a little book about the size of a playing card. We tried taking orders from the kids at school, but the project collapsed due to lack of interest. A Bennett Cerf I was not to be, at least not at eleven.

The surprise of Lennon's book, though, was that it was good. There were similarities to Lewis Carroll's "Jabberwocky," and I enjoyed the silly word play and outlandish drawings. Its small size and $2.50

price tag made it an easy item for young fans to obtain and carry with them, along with their math and spelling texts, around school halls. I didn't bring my copy to school since teachers confiscated them if they caught you reading them in class. The book sold more than 300,000 copies, no mean achievement even for a Beatle. Lennon was asked to speak at an author's luncheon. The dignified, formally dressed literary elite waited expectantly as John mounted the dais. They hoped for pearls to fall from a Beatle's lips. John's entire speech: "Uh, thank you all very much, uh, God bless you." Brian Epstein was there, however, and managed to quell the anger by giving a short talk. It would not be the last time he would have to pour oil on the troubled waters left in Lennon's wake.

The Beatles conquered each medium they attacked. While I sat at my desk, trying to fill my brain with such marvelous things as earth science, sociology, and new math, I listened to the radio as the Beatles poured out one top hit after another—"Can't Buy Me Love," "Twist and Shout," "She Loves You," "I Want to Hold Your Hand," "Please Please Me." During the week of March 21, 1964, they

held twelve positions in the top 100: 1, 2, 3, 4, 5, 16, 44, 49, 69, 74, 84, and 89. Their concerts never failed to stir their audiences. Their records were critical as well as commercial smashes. And now Lennon was making headway into the world of print. There was one field left for them to try: film.

I was growing intrigued by the Beatles. There were stories about them in all the major magazines. They appeared on the covers of *The Saturday Evening Post* and *Life*. Everywhere I turned there was an article or TV news spot showing the latest phase of the craze. And now I would have a chance to watch them act on the big screen.

The release of Richard Lester's *A Hard Day's Night* made history on several fronts. I read that it received a royal premiere in London for which Piccadilly Circus was closed to traffic. The film received almost universal critical acclaim and started the new wave of *cinéma-vérité*. And the stereotypes of Beatle behavior and character, so long touted by the sensational press—John the witty one, Paul the pretty one, George the quiet one, Ringo the one with the nose—were finally crystallized onto celluloid.

Ironically, while expanding these stereotypes, the

(Opposite) Filming A Hard Day's Night: *resting between takes, fighting eager platform crowds, listening to Richard Lester's direction, and coping with a dour Wilfred Brambell. (Above) Lobby card and a scene from a teaser for the film.*

film also presented the Beatles as individuals. Sure, Ringo was good-natured, but he could get angry too. Lennon was sarcastic and unmanageable, but he would show feelings, as he did when trying to cheer up Ringo. Harrison was too often relegated to the background, but his solo scene in the advertising office shows him to be articulate and intelligent. And McCartney was handsome, but he could perform on stage with the best of 'em. According to a cinema teacher I later had in college, "At the time, Lester could have lined the Beatles up against a white wall and filmed them for two hours, and the movie would still have been a hit. As it was, he managed somehow to produce a film that was at once pleasing to the fans and esthetically successful as well."

As I sat in my room, preparing for the class spelling bee or clipping news articles for current events, my mind often wandered to thoughts of what it would be like to be a Beatle, to be mobbed by adoring girls wherever I went. It all seemed very distant. What a fantastic life they must lead, I thought; they're rich, popular, they travel all over the world—how could they possibly be unhappy? When *A Hard Day's Night* came out that summer, though, I found how wrong this image was. Although fictionalized, the film is based on firsthand observations of the Beatles trapped in the hotel during their French tour in January. As I watched, I sensed the boredom, the tediousness of rehearsals, the frightening escapes from fans. It gave me a chance to experience the Beatles on a more personal level, not at the distance generated by concerts or through the remoteness of records. Part of the lasting charm and strong effect of the movie was this sense of reality, the feeling of presence.

Most of this was wasted on the audience I saw the movie with. The girls screamed at every song and at every word the Beatles spoke. No wonder they later complained that they couldn't understand the accents. More than once I had to yell "Shut up!" In 1964 that was a quick way to become unpopular. I left after the matinee was over, blinking in the Saturday afternoon sunshine, feeling very, very happy. The movie made me feel great, and I ran home singing the songs to myself.

The most obvious effect of the film, at least in the school halls, was in language. Liverpudlian slang and catchwords started circulating, and few there were who didn't know what "gear" and "fab" meant. I couldn't use those phrases without sounding self-conscious. I occasionally heard tossed-off phrases like "cum 'ed," "sod off," and "jam buttie." It was a badge of achievement among my peers to be able to quote long passages of dialogue from the movie, and since I had no trouble understanding British accents, I amused my friends by imitating the Beatles' voices. Lines like George's "Ringo's very fussy about his drums; they loom large in his legend," John's falsetto "I now declare this bridge open," and "What are you up to, Ringo?" "Page five," became as much bandied about as "Sock it to me" and "Here come de judge" would be years later.

A Hard Day's Night was released in July in Britain and a month later in the States, but I didn't see

(Opposite) A Hard Day's Night, *though based on the Beatles' touring life, overlooked some of the unhappier aspects of being prisoners of success. Constant travel and media exposure precluded all but the rarest moments of relaxation.* (Above) *Two of the many souvenir books from the film.*

it until after school started again in the fall. I had now entered the seventh grade at Old Mission Junior High. The place seemed like an amazingly vast education machine, grinding out knowledge and maturity like a coffee mill. I felt like a pebble in a fishbowl, small, insignificant, and unnecessary. That year was a national election year; banners and badges started to appear in the hallways bearing the legend, "Ringo for President!"

The Beatles' first major tour of America came close on the heels of the release of *A Hard Day's Night.* Their premiere appearance was in San Francisco on August 19, an event which *The New York Times,* now saturated with Beatlemania, did not see fit to commemorate. But it did not escape the notice of baseball's Charles O. Finley, the flamboyant owner of the Kansas City Athletics (now the Oakland A's), who introduced Kelly-green and gold uniforms to liven up the game. Finley announced, "I'm going to San Francisco to get the Beatles. I promise them to Kansas City and I'm not coming back without them." He flew to San Francisco where he heard the Cow Palace concert. "I thought they were terrific," he said. "I'm not ashamed to say I'm a Beatle fan."

But Kansas City was not on the list of scheduled playdates, and in fact even today September 17 is not mentioned in the official record of concerts other than as a "rest day." That did not deter Charlie O.

(Above) The arrival in America, commemorated by an appropriate backdrop. (Opposite) Airport scenes take on an alarming similarity, whether in New York (top) or hosted by bathing-suited belles in Miami (bottom). Rumor has it that Capitol quietly paid a select few to scream their lungs out.

"I first offered $50,000 to play in our stadium. No answer. I offered $100,000. They said they had several offers of $100,000. So I tore up the check and offered $150,000, because I thought, 'If all those other places are getting the Beatles, how about a break for the Kansas City kids?'"

The $150,000 figure was higher than any ever offered to an artist in America. Later I found out that Brian Epstein, sensing the prestige value of such a contract, had gone to the Beatles, who were playing cards in their dressing room. They didn't even look up when he told them they were going to make almost $5,000 a minute for an additional concert. Epstein was happy: he had his world record; Finley was happy: he had the Beatles.

There was no way Finley could make money on the concert; he didn't plan to. The publicity was his big return. He had pictures taken of himself in a Beatle wig, saying, "Call me Ringo, ha ha." He announced that he would give any money made on the concert to a children's hospital. The tickets for the concert were printed in colors to match the Athletics' uniforms, and on the back there was a picture of Finley in his wig bearing the legend "Today's Beatle's Fans Are Tomorrow's Baseball Fans."

"Personally," said Clarence Kelley, then chief of police in Kansas City, later to become head of the FBI, "I would rather see an invasion from Mars than have to handle the Beatle concert." Nonetheless he arranged to have 350 police at the stadium, plus full medical and communications facilities. Even so, the preparations were ranked only third in magnitude in the city's history—following those made during a flood and a tornado, years earlier.

The Beatles arrived at two o'clock in the morning of the concert, looking pale and tired. I had no interest in being at the airport to meet them. They were whisked away through the rain to the Hotel Muehlebach. The bedsheets they slept on that night were bought by two enterprising businessmen from Chicago, cut into 160,000 square inches, and sold for a dollar each. What is not generally known, however, is that over 100,000 of those souvenirs sit, unsold, in a garage in California. I assume nobody ever tried to bottle Beatle bathwater, but I expect it would have met with a similar lack of success. Not everything the Beatles touched could be turned into gold.

Fewer than half of the 41,000 seats for the Kansas City concert were bought. It pains me now to think how easy it would have been on that night to walk up to the box office, purchase a ticket in any price range, and see the greatest group in the world—an action which, if it should happen by some chance that the Beatles were to give a concert tomorrow, would be roughly equivalent to walking across the Mediterranean in saddle shoes.

Though far from a sellout, the group drew one of the largest crowds on the tour. Kathy Atkinson went, this time on her own initiative, since she had succumbed to Beatlemania after all. Her father bought her the souvenir pennant and program, but he said if she screamed *once* he would take her home. "So we sat," Kathy recalls, "the only two non-screamers in the place." Agnes went, of course, and managed to land on the front page of the *Kansas City Times* the next day, in a photograph of her and other fans, waving their arms and yelling happily.

My sister and her best friend Nancy got to go to the concert that night because they were being escorted by Nancy's father. They didn't want little brothers to tag along, so I wasn't invited. To top it off, it was a Thursday, and I had to take my piano lesson. I was trapped with Bach, Beethoven, and Brahms—the wrong kind of long-hair music. Susie was awfully smug about skipping her lesson and going to the concert, but I tried not to let her triumph register on my face. As she dressed in her junior-high-school jacket and went out the front door into the late-summer air, I felt frustrated and annoyed. Just wait till I'm older, I said to myself; then I'll do whatever I want to do, piano lessons or not.

There is debate over which number the Beatles actually played first during their Kansas City concert on September 17, 1964. One report says it was "Twist and Shout," their standard concert opener; another says it was too noisy to distinguish; while Susie remembers it was "Kansas City." The confusion the Beatles caused is evident in this statement from Bess Coleman, one of the group's press officers:

"When the Beatles played at Kansas City I remember that the Bill Black combo had come on and done their bit, and Jackie de Shannon had done her bit. After the interval the Beatles came on, and their first song was 'Kansas City.' After that the place

(Top left) The Fab Three leave for an equine tour of Central Park. In Miami the boys idle away a well-earned vacation; Ringo looks skeptically out to sea as Paul takes a shaky skiing lesson (left). George, still ill, missed out on the fun but was healthy for the Washington, D.C. concert (opposite bottom).

went completely wild. All the fans broke through all the barriers. Within minutes everybody that was in any seat everywhere was on the pitch [field], and I remember that I was sitting in a caravan with the four Beatles and Derek Taylor. Suddenly the caravan began to rock, and it rocked and rocked and finally we were turned over.

"It's a very fun experience," Bess said in her dry London accent. "I don't know how the caravan was righted, but eventually it was. Police came out, I remember, with truncheons, and I think that was one of the ways they got the fans off the pitch. Derek Taylor had to get up on the stage and sort of yell at the fans through the speakers saying that if you don't sit down again the police are going to cancel this concert. And I don't know how it happened but they all sat down and the concert was finished. At the end the fans broke through everything yet again, and the police had to provide a guard to get the Beatles to the car and away from it all."

The newspapers had a different and more accurate story the next day, however. The front page bore the headline "Police Hold Tide of Beatlemania." There was a report that a few hundred fans *had* rushed to the police line but had only stood waving and yelling good-bye. Certainly there was nothing like the attack on the stage by 20,000 fans that Coleman describes, nor would it be possible for the Beatles to be playing "Kansas City" while seated casually in a caravan. Such are the myths and fallacies of Beatlemania.

My frustration at missing the concert was soon for-

gotten, however. Young wounds are the quickest to heal. I was too busy adjusting to the problems of attending a new school, of learning to calculate a schedule of classes, of living by the bell, and of making new friends. I was struggling with the rigors of Unified Studies, fumbling with the intricacies of metal shop, and dodging the ninth graders in flag football during gym. The problems of grade school were carried over to and amplified in junior high. There were ten times as many students and a hundred times the pressures in getting work done. In the new environment I was even more aware that I still had a lot of growing up to do. The ninth-graders seemed like young adults, tall, well-proportioned, mature. We seventh-graders were still tripping over our own shoelaces. My hands wouldn't take orders, choosing instead to rebel and drop things during the most crowded moments in the halls. My locker was miles away from the nearest classroom and always seemed to jam just as the bell rang.

For respite I joined the "Study Club," a Friday afternoon activity for those who were too shy to sign up for something fun like "Creative Dramatics." I did get a lot of outside reading done there, however, and had my first exposure to the wonders of science fiction during the period. The one place I enjoyed myself most was in music class. I had had good exposure to the classics, church music, songs, and theory, and so I felt a little ahead of the game there. I was even chosen to play "Faith of Our Fathers" on the piano for a seventh-grade class concert—my first

public appearance at the keyboard! Certainly the Beatles had a hand in making me more aware of music and its elements, by stimulating me to listen more carefully to songs than before.

The Beatles preferred, and rightly so, to be judged by their music. The haircuts, the mannerisms, the stereotypes were all fun, but the Beatles were, and are, serious, talented musicians. I can see the origins of their later music in the six albums they released in 1964. "I Want to Hold Your Hand," their first number-one hit in America, is a stirring song. I love its offbeat, fumbling beginning, ecstatic double harmony, and cascading melody line reminiscent of "Please Please Me." It grabs my attention and holds it by shifting from one musical trick to another. Paul's thumping bass and Ringo's surprisingly effective drumming play well off the rhythmic backdrop of hand-claps. John's marvelously sustained wail on the high notes, which was to become his trademark for me in later years, is neatly punctuated by drum riffs and George's murky guitar leads. The tripleted final measures add just the right kick to round out the song and leave me smiling.

Paul the romantic balladeer is present in "Till There Was You," although his arrangement now seems almost humorously over-sentimental to me. George's unusual "Don't Bother Me" prefigures the dark nature of his future songs. I enjoy finding on these early recordings traces of the studio tricks which were soon to lead to so much discussion and furor among my classmates. On both the American

and British LP versions of "Please Please Me," for instance, Lennon bumbles the vocal, saying "why know" instead of "I know," but on the British EP version this mistake was rectified. (An EP is an "extended play" 45-rpm record with four songs on it instead of the usual two. The Beatles released thirteen of these mini-albums in England, but Capitol issued only three in the United States. Today these American EPs are among the most valuable Beatles collector's items.) On "Hold Me Tight," Paul sings "so" and the others sing "now" during the line "It feels so right," a surprise which is really audible only through earphones.

"I Want to Hold Your Hand" and "She Loves You" are my two favorite songs from this early era. For me, though, the best example of the Beatles' songwriting and performing abilities, and the most endearing piece from 1964, is "And I Love Her." I have always preferred acoustic music, which I imagine is a holdover from my classical piano training. The moment in *A Hard Day's Night*, when Paul sings this with George's handsome Spanish-guitar accompaniment, is pure, unadorned pleasure. The simplicity of Ringo's percussion and John's gentle rhythm guitar lets Paul's voice ring out with a sincerity and a double-tracked purity unmatched in any of the ballads from their first year. I can tell that one writer, probably John, had a hand in the middle eight bars, or refrain section. All along they have been singing of "her" and "she," but in the refrain they suddenly shift to "ours" and "you." This is the only flaw in an otherwise perfect gem. The song was later to take on special significance for me, but even at this early stage it made me sense the beauty—and the sorrow—of love.

It is unfortunate that American record companies were more interested in padding their releases than in presenting a quality product. The soundtrack to *A Hard Day's Night* is an example. Included with the eight Beatle songs are four George Martin instrumentals which do not appear on the British version of the album. These instrumentals, however pleasant, break the flow of the music and deprive listeners of a

THE KANSAS CITY STAR

VOL. 81. NO. 366

KANSAS CITY, THURSDAY, SEPTEMBER 17, 1964—38 PAGES

To Subscribe Call HA 1-1200
For Classified Ads Call BA 1-5550

PRICE 7

ED

EP IN POVERTY WAR

se Appropriations Committee Approves 750
Million Dollars for the Administration's
Economic Opportunity Program

NSIT FUNDS

anded Food Stamp
etup Also Is Given
Financing

ashington (AP)—Emer-
y funds totaling almost
llion dollars to finance
poverty war, urban
transit, civil rights
food stamp programs
e approved today by the
se appropriations com-
ee.

e largest allotment was 750
on dollars to start the ad-
tration's anti-poverty, or
mic opportunity, program.
is $197,500,000 less than
dent Johnson requested.

Not as Much Needed

committee noted that the
ram was not approved by
ress as early as the admin-
tion had planned and did
eed the entire amount for
rest of the fiscal year end-
ext June 30.

launch the urban transit
the committee ap-
million dollars of the
requested for grants
agencies to develop
e transportation sys-
150 million denied
been used for ad-
ing for fiscal 1966.
ate agencies

BULLETIN

Sacramento, Calif. (AP)—
President Johnson took the
wraps off today two major defense secrets—radar to give
almost instant warning, and
systems to destroy nuclear-
armed satellites.

This, obviously, was Johnson's reply to claims made by
his Republican rival, Barry
Goldwater, that his administration has failed to provide
any new strategic systems for
meeting a possible Communist
attack.

Johnson, in a speech from
the steps of California's capitol, disclosed the development
of a new radar that "will literally look around the curve of
the earth, alerting us to air-
craft and especially missiles,
within seconds after they are
launched."

The President said the first
over-the-horizon radar units
are being installed. They
mark a major advance over

(Continued on Page 8.)

VOTE CHANGES SEEN BY BARRY

Civil Rights

Fame Wears Thin in Wee Hours . . .

Beatles Arrive, Wan and Harried

AS THE BEATLES PULL AWAY from the Municipal
of young fans strains forward in restrain
roses (center) were upsh
the quartet

'RACE LAW PART V

The Public Accommodations Section of
Rights Act Ruled Unconstitutional by
Judge Federal Panel

UPSET AT CONGRESSIONAL

Concern Over the Spread of Lawmakers
Is Expressed by Jurists—Justice Dep
ment Plans to Appeal

Birmingham, Ala. (AP)—A 3-judge federa
day ruled that the public accommodations sec
civil rights act is unconstitutional as applied
mingham restaurant.

The judges, who expressed their concern
spread of congressional powers, issued a tem
straining order against Nicholas Katzenbac
U. S. attorney general, prohibiting him from
the act.

In Washington, a Justice
department spokesman said
the department will appeal
the decision to the Supreme
court. He said it will ask a
stay of the restraining order granted by the 3-judge
court, pending disposition
of the case by the high
court.

The ruling, filed in U. S. district court here, was in connec-
n with a suit brought by Ollie
ar, and his son, co-
arbecue.

Soviet Uses Ve in United N

United Nations (
Soviet Union today
Norwegian resoluti
ing the September
of Indonesia-based
on Malaysian territ

The vote in the
council was 9-2 w
viet Union and
Czechoslovakia vet
it. This was the
cast by the Russia
first in more than

BRITISH REP
LANDINGS BY
PAGE 6

THE KANSAS CITY TIMES, FRIDAY, SEPTEMBER 18, 1964

ce Hold Tide of Beatlemania

BEATLEMANIA IN KANSAS CITY—Appeared thus last night as 20,208 screaming spectators—m
cheered their idols during a 31-minute performance at the Municipal Stadium. Many of the girls
formance was over. Four other acts took up the rest of the 2-hour show.

but considerably short of
$150,000.

Finley said he was delighted
with the performance and that
he considered the behavior of
Kansas City teen-agers indeed
commendable. He praised the
work of the police and of U.
M. K. C. and Rockhurst college students who acted as
ushers.

So, concerning the physical
aspects—the security, the
traffic, the crowds—all went
well. Reason prevailed.

Some Worn Out

But the event left some of
the Beatle followers emotionally torn. As the crowds left
the park, fully 10 minutes after all the shouting, there

were groups of exhausted
girls still seated in the playing
field area and the stands.
They were crying.

Why?

"Because they (the B's)
just left and didn't say anything," a girl explained, rub-
bing her eyes. "Now they are
gone forever."

"Ah, they'll be back again,"
a policeman said.

"What do you care?" the
girl wept. "You were down in
front there and you didn't
care and I was way back here
and I couldn't even get close
to them."

"Now wait a minute, ho-
ney," he said. "It's not my
fault."

Then he walked away.
Ear Stoppers Needed

Many of the policemen w
manned the barricade in
of the blaring loudspe
put cotton in their ea
others not so well t
the sound of the ma
—a fearful sound
seems out of
linger, not gen
memory.

The Beatle
sant beat an
of electric
volume lim
on jukeboxes
thousand joints
stores. The scream
volume control.

Scarlett Peterson, 14,

VOL. 97. NO. 10

The Ka

Police Hold Tide of Beatle

KANSAS

YELLING, SCREAMING AND WAVING, fans of the Beatles had their night
four long-tressed British singers performed. The fans also did a great deal of
though most of the fans were teen-age girls, the young man at left got into the
rose in Municipal Stadium and
hundreds of flashbulbs lit the
park like harsh fireflies.

The scream tore on and on.
The performers, jolly and
jaunty, sounded some practice
guitar chords, said "Ha"
into the microphones
and abruptly ripped into a

tune called "Twist and
Shout."

The scream, from an au-
dience of 20,230, reached frightening intensity. A man
smoking a cigar in the front
row put his hands over his
ears and puffed.

The Beatles played for 31

[ADDITIONAL STORIES AND
PICTURES ON PAGE 3, 6 AND 30.]

By Robert K. Sanford
(A Member of The Star's Staff)
HEN the announcer
said, "The Beatles,"
and the four British
singers bounced onto
the stage a concerted scream

minutes, 12 songs perha
and only as they left did
screaming die, sinking in
mournful moan.

"They are gone, gone
Girl said, "I'll never see t
again."

And so the night of the
(Continued on Page 8

front-row seat was
chell, 15, of 7205 Fl
president of the I
lies spelled in
Kansas City
thought the s
and she had
A friend
cle, 14, of
vard, h
ship of
Paul
at th
enc

don, chairman
members
(Bert) Bates
arold H. Crogh
frank Ellis; Davi
Jerzy Hauptmann
Ingram; Cliff C.
P. LeVota; the R
Middleton; John P
ert Rhoades, wor
Clair H. Schroede
Shutz; Stuart Wien
Willcox

staff
ivate inc
financed

DI AZA
LIBRARY
OSED
Long-Haired Quartet
Concert Is a Classic

NOTIONS

SCHOOL ACT
PLAN OUT

CHARLES O. FINLEY
IS PLEASED TO PRESENT .. FOR THE ENJOYMENT
OF THE BEATLE FANS IN MID-AMERICA
"THE BEATLES"
IN PERSON
THURSDAY, SEPTEMBER 17, 1964 — 8:00 P.M.
RAIN OR SHINE - NO REFUNDS
MUNICIPAL STADIUM   UPPER DECK BOX SEAT $6.50
KANSAS CITY, MO.   82

...OR THE ENJOYMENT
...FANS IN MID-AMERICA
...HE BEATLES"
IN PERSON
...HURSDAY, SEPTEMBER 17, 1964 — 8:00 P.M.
RAIN OR SHINE - NO REFUNDS
...NICIPAL STADIUM LOWER DECK BOX SEAT
...NSAS CITY, MO.   82
$6.50

YEAH YEAH! YEAH!
TODAY'S BEATLE'S FANS
ARE
TOMORROW'S BASEBALL FANS

Charles O. Finley
PRESIDENT

(Opposite) The airport crowd was small for the rainy 2 a.m. arrival of the Beatles in Kansas City. (Above) No concert was scheduled for KC; Finley bought the Beatles' day off, losing money on the deal but winning immortality in the press and through the gag photo on the souvenir ticket.

more unified experience. English releases usually contain fourteen songs per album, whereas their American counterparts had as few as ten. Songs released as singles seldom appeared on the British LPs; American companies stretched one song onto as many as eight different records.

The release of *Beatles '65* at the end of the year allows us to detect what gargantuan strides the Beatles had made in their music since the beginning. From the raw, tatty recordings of such minor, uninspired efforts like "Baby It's You" and "Misery" came the beauty and harmony of well-conceived numbers like "No Reply," "I'll Follow the Sun," "She's a Woman," and "I Feel Fine." Their experimentation with instrumentation, which began with the captivating use of John's wailing harmonica and culminated at the end of 1964 with a variety of keyboards, shows their willingness to seek new and fresher forms of expressing their increasingly complex musical ideas. The Beatles never stood still. Since I played piano, I especially appreciated the Beatles' use of the instrument. All my other friends were learning guitar or drums, so I was glad for the nod the Beatles gave us struggling Van Cliburns.

The coming of Christmas was, as usual, a time of retrospection. My family took time to consider all the blessings of the past year. I looked at photos in the scrapbook and saw that I had grown quite a bit—and my hair, though still slicked back on Sundays, was considerably longer than it had ever been.

The first year of the Beatles and Beatlemania in America will always be the best year of my youth. I remember the fun they generated, the sense that something outside my world was happening. The Beatles were the one thing that we all had in common—love them or hate them, you couldn't ignore them. I recall the joy on the faces of my friends, and the playful but real annoyance of those who didn't understand or appreciate the Beatles. "Beatles 4-Ever!" was the happy battlecry of an entire generation. I would have found myself growing up eventually, I suppose, but the Beatles made me more aware of myself and of a world going on around me. As I passed my twelfth birthday, I reached the years of a new maturity, of a slowly growing sense of love and sexuality. I found that Beatle songs expressed the hurts and the happinesses of those twelve years. The loneliness of a shy preteen was echoed in songs like "No Reply," and "I'm a Loser." My awareness of the wonderful and strange thing called Woman was reflected in "All My Loving," "I Saw Her Standing There," and "She Loves You." The Beatles sang to me, taking my joy and my pain and explaining it to me in terms I could understand. Without them, memories of the past would be a silent black-and-white film; the Beatles give my past color and sound —and meaning.

1965

. . . when the radio kept us all in tune
and help was never far away
and we felt fine eight days a week . . .

In 1965 astronauts were going into outer space, soldiers were going to Vietnam, and I was going crazy trying to survive the stress of minor-league scholarship. I must have succeeded, because my yearbook is signed with such endearments as "From a dumb 7th-grader to a smart one" and "Thanks for helping me in study hall when I needed it."

My yearbook photo shows me wearing a white shirt and bolo tie, a string tie with a glass slide in which was encased a real, but dead, scorpion. My hair is longer, but arched to one side. Any wayward strands are kept in place by a liberal dose of Wildroot Creme Oil. My forehead is shiny, still unplagued by adolescent acne. Such an unblemished record was too good to last.

The cover of the Old Mission Junior High School yearbook (named "The Panther" after our mascot) shows a snarling feline leaping from a spacecraft, two things that symbolize my whole year. When I wasn't at school, trying to cope with the conjugation of French verbs or learning how to bolt two pieces of wrought iron together, I was following the Gemini, Ranger, and Mariner space missions with a fervor approaching that of the Beatle fans. I clipped each space article that appeared and filed it away in a scrapbook. I knew all the astronauts by name and even sharpened my pencils in a capsule-shaped sharpener. The blast-offs were usually nicely timed so that I could watch them before going to school. I knew I could never become an astronaut, since space heroes don't wear glasses, but I vowed to myself that someday I would walk on the moon.

Reading gave weight to my daydreams. I discovered volumes by H. G. Wells and Jules Verne in the library, and was snared by science fiction. I rushed through my homework in study hall so I'd have time to read *First Men in the Moon* or *The Mysterious Island*.

The other guys were more concerned with the upcoming baseball season or with endless speculations about whom they would take to the school party. The girls, of course, had the same concern about parties. They may have been dedicated to the Beatles, but they knew John Lennon was never going to drop from the clouds and ask them to dance.

That didn't stop them from hoping, however. While I dreamed of spaceships and submarines, the girls I knew dreamed of Beatles. Debbie, a friend, remembers skipping school with her classmates to go downtown and await the release of the latest teenage magazines, each crammed with "fab pix and stories" of the group. They took them home to the basement, where they squealed over each new photograph. "I

(Opposite) The Beatles conquered the Establishment when they received medals as MBEs. (Above) Meanwhile my brother Robert had just joined the Cub Scouts and I, conspicuously medal-less, was struggling to advance past the rank of Tenderfoot.

syllables while you're saying it.

I'd often heard about "locker room talk" but had never experienced it. On my first day in gym class, however, I learned several four-letter words that I'm *sure* my grandmother never used. As I got dressed in my little white T-shirt, jock strap, and gym shorts, I realized I would probably learn more in the locker room than I would in class. I also felt a tiny sliver of fear run up my spine that told me there was going to be much more to life than Saturday-morning cartoons and stuffed toys.

There's an old saying that goes "He who laughs last didn't get the joke." It's true. Many times a voice would shout something over the gym lockers at which the guys would roar with laughter, while I stood there puzzled. I always went to Rick, who explained it all to

The Beatles kept their spirits high despite rigorous touring schedules. (Opposite) Rented juke boxes and hired bands blasted out Beatle tunes at junior high parties and gave inspiration to countless amateur talent show routines.

wasn't a screamer," Debbie recalls. "I cried instead. It wasn't just a crush; I *was in love* with John Lennon. Paul was too pretty, and my friends and I decided George looked like he had bad breath."

The Beatles triggered emotional releases these adolescent girls had never felt before. The younger ones felt tremors of ecstasy at concerts but didn't know why. The older ones *did* know why, however. Thirteen- and fourteen-year-olds, just discovering their own sexuality, could direct their sexual energies toward the Beatles. Some psychiatrists declared that the Beatles were a non- or presexual attraction, but the girls I know tell me differently. Debbie remembers her friends staring at photographs of the Beatles in tight pants and ogling at them.

Sex, for me, was still as mysterious as a ship in a bottle. I knew it was there, but I didn't know how it got there or what it was for. Rick and I had stared eagerly at a few tattered copies of *Playboy*, smuggled furtively between our houses under our jackets, and I had felt strange stirrings within me. Somehow, though, I never really made the connection between the glossy, waxen, airbrushed beauties in the pictures and the chunky, braces-wearing, awkward girls in my class. My body was going through those changes that eventually plague and excite everyone. I was proud of the little hairs that curled tentatively forth from hidden recesses. My voice started trying to find its range, but it seemed to experiment at all the wrong moments. Just try explaining to your parents, "I'm old enough to stay up late," when your voice jumps a quick octave between

Our Parties

BZZZ

BEATLES

me. I remember standing on my front porch while he patiently disclosed everything he knew, using his hands to form little models of the things he described. I listened wide-eyed. "Really?" I said in astonishment at the end of each sentence. *"Really?"* After our session I felt like a frustrated graduate with a degree in philosophy: a lot of theoretical knowledge with no chance for practical application.

The Boy Scouts also served a great function as disseminators of this type of information, although I'm sure Baden-Powell didn't have that in mind as its primary goal. I had joined Troop 95 the year before, and spent one weekend a month roughing it on camp-outs with the Beaver patrol. Rick was also in the troop. It was nice to have a close friend to share scouting with. We had even occupied the same tent at camp the sum-

mer before. On camp-outs, as usual, he explained to me any dirty joke that passed in the dark from sleeping bag to sleeping bag. Within our canvas tents, the glow from official Boy Scout flashlights illuminated many a page of *Playboy*. No one seemed interested in looking at the science-fiction books I brought along.

Those fifty-cent space-race paperbacks were about all I could afford to buy. My income was limited to my weekly allowance, which had just been raised from fifteen cents to a quarter, hardly enough to cover the cost of Beatle records. My sister could afford an occasional single, however, so I had to be satisfied with what she bought. To keep us interested in the piano my father gave us some popular sheet music, among which was a volume called *The Beatle Book of Recorded Hits*. It was one of the first books of their music to come out,

since it contained such gems as "My Bonnie" and "Sweet Georgia Brown." Fortunately, though, the radio was an easily accessible form of entertainment for me, and the Beatles were there at every turn of the knob.

Following the success of "She's a Woman" and "I Feel Fine," a two-sided hit, the Beatles released "Eight Days a Week"/"I Don't Want to Spoil the Party" in the middle of February. I think "Eight Days" has one of the best rhythms and melodics of all Beatle songs and is a wonderfully well-arranged piece. Its fanfare beginning excited me each time I heard it on the radio. "I Don't Want to Spoil the Party" began to give me an inkling that all is not always right, even in the world the Beatles were creating. There was rejection and loneliness, there was even the bitterness caused by alcohol. The singer has had a drink or two and doesn't care, and leaves the party to look for his missing girl, leaving instructions to let him know if she turns up.

The emotional depth of that particular song didn't strike me until I was a little older, but I understood what the song was saying. I went to the parties the school sponsored, but being far too young to date, I went alone. I probably would have run like a scared snipe if I'd had to ask a girl out. My parents encouraged me to go, saying, "All the girls will want you to be there. They'll miss you if you don't go."

"They won't either," I replied.

I was right.

Parties in junior high were semitraumas for the unprepared. A noisy, third-rate band was hired to play third-rate versions of popular songs. Streamers of crepe paper theoretically turned the gymnasium into a veritable fantasyland, but the effort was seldom worth it: It was still a gym, and it still smelled of sweaty sneakers. The older, braver kids danced occasionally; mostly, however, everyone hung around the concession table set up in the multipurpose room. The yearbook immortalized these parties with photos of girls playing Ping-Pong, boys bent over their chess sets, and a sparsely populated dance floor.

Susie recalls that in the girls' room during the parties a friend of hers recited scenes from *A Hard Day's Night*, complete with accents, while other girls tried to outboast each other by recounting the number of times they'd seen the film. Meanwhile the band in the gym was butchering "Can't Buy Me Love," "Twist and Shout," and "Rock 'n' Roll Music."

I returned from the parties a little depressed. I knew it was considered "uncool" (or "unflash," "flash" being the new teen word from England to replace "fab" and "gear") to play Ping-Pong all night, but it was beyond me even to think of dancing such jerking gymnastic oddities as the frug, the twist, and the pony. I tried once or twice, since with those dances you didn't even have to be within a city block of your partner, but resigned myself to an evening of roaming the halls and watching the people.

During school every move the Beatles made was subject for discussion among the girls. The paper reported things that would have gone unnoticed if done by ordinary mortals. Such newsworthy items as the results of John's driver's test (successful) and the theft of Paul's car by his mechanic (unsuccessful) were faith-

(Opposite) The Beatles were crowd-pleasers, and fans responded by showering them with gifts. Besides portraits, Ringo received thousands of rings in the mail. (Above) Typical Beatle souvenirs.

fully announced by the wire services.

Slightly more earthshaking was the front-page news that Ringo married Maureen Taylor on February 11, 1965. The lucky girl, an eighteen-year-old, dark-haired beautician from Liverpool, was described by Walter Shenson, producer of *A Hard Day's Night*, as "a very charming, quiet little girl, and deeply in love with Ringo. And Ringo is deeply in love with her." The ceremony was performed in the Caxton Hall Registry Office, whose janitor acted as witness. Beatles manager Brian Epstein was best man. The wedding was captured in a series of beautiful photographs by the Beatles' official shutterman, Robert Freeman.

Two down and two to go. Now the only unmarried ones were Paul and George. When the news of Ringo's wedding broke, some girls felt betrayed, cheated, hurt. Others went on blithely ignoring the fact, as they did with John Lennon's wife. It made no difference to them whether their "faves" were married or not. "I'll get you in the end," they seemed to say.

By now I was beginning to grow a little tired of the whole thing, though by no means because of any fault of the Beatles or their music. Constant media exposure began to get boring and to wear down the novelty for me. Beatle souvenirs, bracelets, necklaces, games, books, and magazines swamped dime store display tables until I wanted to scream. Besides, I had other, more important things to do than worry about Ringo's marriage or Paul's car. I remember being irked with some girl who started crying in French class because "now I'll never get to marry Ringo."

"So what?" I replied, ducking the textbook she threw at me.

Some of the tremors of apathy I started feeling toward the group stemmed from the fact that the Beatles spawned such a plethora of would-be imitators. Gimmickry all too often substituted for talent. There was

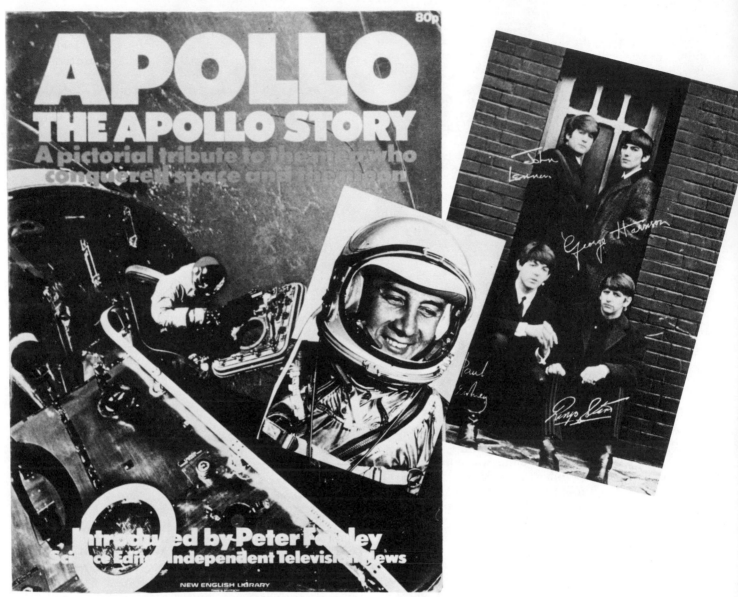

actually a group that called itself The Undertakers, who rode around London on motorcycles wearing black mourning jackets which they swung over their heads at the conclusion of their act. Whoopee. There were groups who wore bizarre costumes and makeup that make Alice Cooper look like Shirley Temple, and groups with odd names like The Swinging Blue Jeans. Indeed. And of course they all wore long hair.

Occasionally a group came along with a little more talent, like the Dave Clark Five and Gerry and the Pacemakers, whose songs I really enjoyed. Petula Clark's "Downtown," one of a handful of popular records reviewed that year in the *Kansas City Star*, was mentioned as "a portent of better things to come in teenage music." I thought the song was great and really captured everything I felt about the beat of the city.

To teenagers with money to spend on records and fan magazines it made little difference who the group was. Debbie's Beatles scrapbook is even titled "The Beatles —or Anything Else from *England*." The Dave Clark Five, fomenters of the so-called Tottenham Sound (as distinct from the Mersey Sound) made the front page of London newspapers when their hit "Glad All Over" replaced the Beatles in the number-one spot. "The

reign of King Beatle may be over," reported *News of the World*. But after seeing a concert by Billy J. Kramer and the Dakotas, Debbie, in a wonderfully incisive observation, wrote in her diary: "The funny thing about these performances is that after each performance you could swear you will never love another group besides the one you just saw. Then, in a couple of days, after it all wears off, you go back to loving the Beatles again."

Not everyone loved the Beatles, however. A child-guidance expert, Dr. Bernard Saibel, reported that a Beatles concert was an orgy for teenagers, a "destructive process" in which teenagers became "frantic, hostile, uncontrollable, screaming, unrecognizable beings, possessed by some demonic urge." Publishing such reports could get you in big trouble. Letter columns in the newspapers were filled with attacks on Beatles critics, calling them "creatures from the Twilight Zone," "out of their minds," inconsiderate, cruel, mean, stupid, foolish. Charlie Rice, syndicated humorist, wrote that because of a misunderstood comment on the Beatles, he received letters calling him a "worm," an "unutterable Skunk," an "insult to the human race," "the world's stupidest square," "an insect." "Of all the low, slithering snakes that crawl the earth," read one letter, "you are preeminent!"

An anti-Communist group, the Christian Crusade, denounced the Beatles in a pamphlet called *Communism, Hypnotism, and the Beatles.* "Beatles music," it read, "will hypnotize American youth and prepare them for future submission to subversive control. Music of the Beatles, like other innocuous-sounding rhythms heard daily by American children, is in actuality part of a systematic plan geared to making a generation of American youth mentally ill and emotionally unstable; a scientific plan geared to using the destructive qualities of music for the degeneration of American youth."

The Beatles' power reached from the humblest bespectacled, gangly teenager to the highest people in the world. The weekly newspaper of the Vatican suggested that there was more hair than talent in the Beatles' imitators: "Not all of the four-man groups have adequate talent at their disposal and thus, where their throats could not take them, their hair did. And the hysterical girls who love to frequent the performances of the present-day singers exalt them as much for the wig as for the voice. But at least the idea of the first four hairy ones was original." The newspaper's advice to the new groups: "Buy a farm and listen to the song of crowing roosters and cackling hens."

It was even reported that the Beatles failed to make the Top 10 in Red China, losing out to songs like "Ho Chi Minh—The Most Beautiful Name in Vietnam," "U.S. Imperialists Get Out of Vietnam," and "Long Live Algeria."

On the home front personal clashes over the group were common. I heard someone accuse Rick of growing his hair long "just so you'll look like the Beatles." I had trouble persuading my father to let my hair grow longer in back, and often during our haircutting sessions in the basement I squealed and squirmed because he was too energetic with the clippers. School officials were ret-

icent to admit that a new era had come. High schools with swimming pools ruled that boys with long hair had to wear bathing caps. The administration put pressure on the Old Mission student congress to pass a controversial hair and dress code. Any student with hair past a certain length (collar, ears—the rules were arbitrary) could be expelled. I never had to worry, though. When it came to experimenting with fashion, I was about as quick to pick things up as Venus de Milo.

Here was what some saw as the key issue at the heart of Beatlemania. The Beatles represented something that was exclusively "teenage." They did not belong to the adults. As Dr. Saibel put it, "Every time a teenager screams over this music, he thumbs his nose with impunity at an adult." Perhaps there *was* something rebellious about it all. Perhaps if parents had acquiesced to the new hair styles and fashions without hesitation, the thrill would have gone. From my seventh-grade standpoint, though, it seemed the "revolution," if that word can be used, was natural. It just so happened that the Beatles were coincidentally at one end of it, conveniently placed to receive both the praise and the blame.

About this time my world was expanding considerably. The Beatles united me with all teenagers; they were something held in common by all of us. I became more aware of myself both as an individual and as one of a generation. I still watched television heavily, and as summer approached I settled for reruns of Red Skelton, Jack Benny, "Combat!" and "Shindig"—"the only TV show louder than its commercials." I remember seeing a Cara Williams show in which she imagined she was a bigger singing star than the Beatles, and a "Petticoat Junction" episode in which the

(Opposite) For a while I was more interested in America's space program than in the Beatles. (Below) John gives Paul a "thumbs up" as he successfully completes his driver's license test.

three daughters wore wigs and formed a group called "The Ladybugs." "The Beverly Hillbillies" never excited me, and the subtle humor of "The Man From U.N.C.L.E." escaped me. "The Fugitive" was still running, and Alfred Hitchcock showed his corpulent profile each week.

My parents took me to see *Mary Poppins*, which gave me a headache. *My Fair Lady* played almost the entire year of 1965 in Kansas City, and I remember reading the movie ads and wishing the film would just go away. *Goldfinger* was the biggie, though. It had come out the year before, and you were nobody until you'd seen it. My father took the three of us kids to see *Go Go Mania* at the Fairway Theatre, the same place where *A Hard Day's Night* had played. This was an odd little film, featuring the top groups of the year (Beatles, Animals, Herman's Hermits, and so on). Each one got up in front of the camera and sang one or two numbers, lip-synched, and accented by tacky studio lighting. I recall girls screaming when "Herman" (Peter Noone) smiled his extremely toothy grin. (Her-

man told a press conference he got letters such as the one enclosing a stick of gum with the instructions "Chew once and send back to me and I'll chew it for the rest of my life.")

On the radio I listened to Bob Dylan's songs without any particular relish. I thought he was a lousy singer and a worse harmonica player but that his songs—"Mr. Tambourine Man," "Blowin' in the Wind," and "It Ain't Me Babe"—were pretty when done by other people. Herb Alpert's Tijuana Brass put out bouncy little records, and I remember Susie practicing her audition for the ninth-grade drill team to the music of "Spanish Flea." "The House of the Rising Sun" was a smash. School bands still played "Gloria," "96 Tears," "Little Latin Lupe Lu," "California Girls," and "Surfin' U.S.A." as well as the notorious "Louie Louie," in either the clean or the pornographic version. One of my

(Above) Ringo's drums beat time for the group, but his heart was beating for the lovely Maureen Cox (opposite), his Liverpudlian bride and joy.

(Above) The Beatles and the Merseyside Class of 1964. These performers, including Cilla Black and P. J. Proby, were all members of Brian Epstein's stable of talent and accompanied the Beatles on several of their tours. Other chart-toppers of the era were the surprisingly innocent-looking Rolling Stones (left) and opposite, reading left to right and down: Gerry and the Pacemakers, a bearish Manfred Mann and crew, the Dave Clark Five, the Swinging Bluejeans, and Herman's Hermits.

favorites was "Do Wah Diddy Diddy" by Manfred Mann.

Capitol Records released an album of very early Beatle songs in April of 1965. This was a part of that incredible effort to cash in on their popularity, since the songs had variously appeared on six other albums on different labels. A strange thing was happening about this time. Budget records on obscure labels were released, advertised as Beatle albums ("strictly long-hair music") but containing only one or two Beatle cuts. Other albums featured Beatle look-alikes doing Beatle songs, with tricky covers or misleading cover-copy wording. Complaints on this score led to an investigation of the matter by the New York State attorney general. I remember walking into a discount store and seeing a new album with huge red letters spelling BEAT!! and photos of four moptops and a deceiving design that would easily have fooled a casual observer. I was mad to think I almost bought the thing. Hundreds of poor teenagers had probably been taken in and had unknowingly dished out their cherished allowance dollars

for cheap leftovers.

My teachers were observing the effect of Beatle music on their students. We had some fairly young teachers at Old Mission, and I was delighted when one of them got up in front of class and started singing a Dave Clark Five song. For the school talent show three faculty members donned mop heads to do a parody on the Beatles, and some students did the inevitable mime to a scratchy 45-rpm single. A school in Michigan ordered $2,000 worth of classical records as an "antidote" to the Beatles. The claim was made that "The Beatles have given kids the idea that only the banjo and percussion are important." Faulty claim there. The Beatles *never* used banjo on any of the recordings they released.

The Rolling Stones were coming into increasing prominence. They were notorious for their scruffy, violent image. One of their 1965 albums' notes read, "Thrust deep into your pocket for loot to buy this disc of grooves and fancy words. If you don't have bread, see that blind man, knock him on the head, steal his wallet and behold, you have the loot. If you put in the boot, good. Another one sold." Sounds like *A Clockwork Orange*, doesn't it? My sister bought the Stones' singles like "Get Off My Cloud" and "Satisfaction," but I couldn't stand (or understand) them. The Stones were everything the Beatles weren't. They were dirty and obnoxious but, mysteriously, very popular. They

were the rockers who challenged the whole gamut of Beatle-spawned "mod" groups. The Beatles even wrote a song for Mick Jagger to sing, "I Wanna Be Your Man." After that there was to be a great deal of vying for attention and creative success between the two.

"Ticket to Ride" was released on April 19, and it went straight to the number-one spot that week. The single was rushed out so quickly that the label still said, "From the United Artists Release 'Eight Arms to Hold You,'" which Paul thought was a "crummy title." It was changed to *Help!*, of course, just before the movie was released. "Ticket" indicates the new level of maturity the group had reached. Lennon, always strong, was now even stronger. The relationship between the boy and the girl in the song is one of living together, certainly more advanced than holding hands or being happy just to dance. And I couldn't understand the damn thing for the longest time. Ticket to ride what? To where? I began to feel that I was losing touch with the group, that they were getting too far ahead of me. I was aware that even though I was already in seventh grade I still had miles to go.

Beatles VI marked the beginning of summer 1965. Although I still didn't buy records, I did listen to Rick's copies. I especially enjoyed "Words of Love" because of its slurred harmonies and vocal "oohs" and "aahs," and "Every Little Thing," with its magnificent beat and tympani-like refrain rhythm. The Beatles scored a

direct hit by recording a version of "Kansas City." The kids in the Midwest were grateful for the nod given them by the most influential foursome since Matthew, Mark, Luke, and John. It made me feel as if Kansas City *did* exist after all and was not just a cow town. The song received heavy air play although it was not a single until Capitol released it later as an oldie.

In June came the famous announcement that the Beatles were to be invested with memberships in the Most Excellent Order of the British Empire for "services to export." A dozen or so medals were returned in protest by former recipients, but the decision to honor the group stood. This put the cap on the Beatles' acceptance by the adult world. Oh sure, the occasional howl of denunciation still reverberated from the lunatic fringe, but if the *queen* said okay—well, who's to argue? We teenagers had the weight of royal support behind our idols, and who could buck a thousand years of tradition?

After the investiture ceremony, which was staged in October, the Beatles recalled their experience at Buckingham Palace. They admitted to smoking pot in the Royal Bathroom to help them over their nervousness.

(Opposite and above) The Beatles' second trip to America: crowds, planes, visits with fans and celebrities like Don Rickles. (Left) My family also toured the country, covering more routine attractions like New York's natural history museum.

(Opposite) These photos from 1964 apply to every Beatle tour: endless press conferences, rehearsals, hotels, and awards. (Above) Brian Epstein proudly displays his boys' first album and attends rehearsal for the 1965 Ed Sullivan appearance.

They giggled throughout the rehearsal, and the man assigned to the task of calling out each name kept breaking into laughter whenever he reached "Ringo Starr." John drew a blank when the queen asked casually what the Beatles had been up to during the last year, and Ringo, when asked by Her Majesty how long they'd been together, replied amiably, "Forty years." Later Ringo told a reporter that "being MBEs hasn't changed us. You needn't stay on your knees." I didn't really understand the significance of the award, but I knew that the band had been hobnobbing with the queen and that was good enough for me.

Ironically, just as the Beatles were being cited by Her Majesty for generating income for the United Kingdom, an article appeared in the *Kansas City Times* headlined "Pop! Goes the Beatles Fad," reporting that album and single sales had dropped by about $1.3 million by April of 1965, and that dance halls were converting back from pop bands to traditional dance groups. How fleeting is success, and how anxious the press is to find signs of its passing. *Who's Who*, however, decided that the Beatles had proved their staying power over other flash-in-the-pan groups, and they were slated to be included in the 1966-67 edition. And

it was revealed that British soldiers were no longer required to keep their hair cut short. "The day of the military crop is over," announced the army secretary. A former sergeant major complained, "I've never heard anything so silly. If the army goes to these long-haired, modern hair styles, the lads won't be able to hear their orders!"

The Beatles' 1965 summer American tour schedule was revealed, but Kansas City was not to be included this time. It looked as though Charlie Finley had had enough and was not willing to carry Kansas City teenagers' standard into battle a second time at a personal cost of $150,000. This tour was better organized, and though shorter it made even more money than the last. The souvenir program sold during the 1965 concerts had ads for the "London Look (Self-realization means His Capitulation)" by Yardley Cosmetics, Rickenbacher guitars, and London Fog coats. Interestingly, the inside pages carry no pictures of the Beatles as a group, only as individuals.

The story of the tour was the same as in 1964. More hysteria, more fans won over, more head-shaking and tongue-clucking by uncomprehending over-thirty's. My summer, though, was more relaxed. Unhampered by the chores of schoolwork (I burned my metal shop notebook as a vent for my vehemence against the class), I spent my days lolling by the side of the pool at the Homestead Country Club. My parents had just joined, but I felt out of place among all those new people.

(Opposite and above) Paul, one of two bachelor Beatles, rocked fans with the announcement of his engagement to Jane Asher. (Below) John's 1965 book and some early sheet music.

(Above and opposite) Help!, *the Beatles' second film, was funny and fast-moving, but the boys sometimes seemed confused as to what was going on.*

Never much of a swimmer, I stood poolside like a shivering, shrunken salamander, not daring to dive in for fear of turning as blue as my swim trunks. I usually passed up the pleasures of dunking myself in ice-cold water for the drier joy of lying in the sun and indulging my taste (now an addiction) for science fiction. I had even begun my own first novel toward the end of the school year, a terrible thing called *The World That Time Forgot.* Catchy, eh? *I* should have forgotten it. It was all one Verne-inspired cliché, complete with dinosaurs, giant ants, and bad writing. I had devoted my entire study hall to churning out six pages of pencil-written, smudgy manuscript each hour but didn't finish it until summer set me and my imagination free. I set my goal at three hundred pages and, by golly, when I reached it I ended the book, right there.

My family took a trip east to the New York World's Fair, where I worshiped at the Lincoln exhibit in the Illinois Pavilion and gazed myopically at Sinclair Oil's dinosaur replicas. New York was undergoing a severe water shortage at the time—in some restaurants you could still get water free, but they charged you a dime for the glass.

I was in New York a month before the Beatles played their famous Shea Stadium concert, on August 15, 1965. They arrived in New York the day before, and the paper commented on the front page that it didn't look as though the Beatles had been to the barber since the last time they were here. The article pointed out that the Beatles were to perform from Shea's second base—farther than the Mets, the "losingest team in baseball," had gotten all season. The day of the concert, while rioting flared in the Watts district of Los Angeles, McCartney announced his plans to marry Jane Asher, an eighteen-year-old actress. If the announcement lost Paul or the group any fans, it wasn't very obvious, as more than 55,000 Beatle people came to the stadium to hurl themselves at the feet of their idols.

The concert is a landmark in the Beatles' story. Even the Fab Four admitted it was about the best concert they had done. The performance was filmed and was to be shown on television the next year. The logistics of organization were even more complicated than they were during the previous tour. In a "Man from U.N.C.L.E." move the police coordinated the smuggling of the Beatles from downtown to the stadium by armored van and helicopter. A chief of police from Georgia was there to observe techniques that might come in handy when the Beatles arrived in Atlanta. "We want to be ready to handle any unusual situation that may come up," he said.

The summer of 1965 was a busy one for the Beatle boys. John's second book, *A Spaniard in the Works,*

"You can use my phonograph, but I'm not going to buy your records for you. So there." And that was the end of the matter. I didn't buy *Help!* until almost four years later.

I had fallen in love with *Help!*'s cartoon imagery, the dazzling use of color and slapstick gags. Today, however, the film seems to pale for me in comparison with *A Hard Day's Night.* The exotic locales were backdrops which swallowed up the Beatles. Ironically, fantasy worked less well in generating Beatle mythology than the stark, black-and-white documentary technique of the earlier work. Director Richard Lester had been restricted by his bosses: no Beatles performing, no Beatles drinking or smoking or going with girls. In other words, no work and no play makes Beatles a little dull, right? He had to be content with using the Beatles as minor players in their own film, puppets to whom things merely happened. (As far as the "no sex" rule goes, the innuendos of the scene in which Paul plays a girl like a guitar were not lost on the female audience. Debbie remembers thrilling when Paul "accidentally" touches the girl's breast and smiles for a brief second.) *Help!* is jolly great entertainment but glossy and a bit hollow. That's forgivable. It's still Beatles.

The advent of winter brought new changes, both to the Beatles and to my feelings about them, and to my world in general. Eighth grade was near the brink of high school, which made it even more terrifying than the seventh grade had been. The Beatles released *Rubber Soul* during the first week of December, but I wasn't aware of it until early in 1966. Nineteen sixty-five was a year of repeats for the Beatles—another film, another Lennon book, another concert tour, more good albums, the same mania that followed them from the first. I was growing older; I got more out of their music than ever before, but at the same time I was aware that there was a lot I was missing. As my sense of personal values matured, I found myself at war with the Beatles. We were about to have a parting of the ways.

came out in June. *Help!*, the Beatles' second film, was released a month later. When an interviewer asked what the boys were up to, they replied in typical Beatle fashion. Paul said he and John were writing a musical; George said he and Ringo had "painted Buckingham Palace." "Green with black shutters," added the Nose. Paul said he had the lead in a new Tarzan film. "It offers me full scope for my acting and physical abilities." Not to be outdone, George then declared he was now "fullback for a soccer team." Asked to comment on the "taste of American fans," Paul answered, "Don't know. Haven't bitten any."

I went to the premiere of *Help!* in Kansas City on August 18 at the Uptown Theatre. I was quickly learning the prestige value of being "the first one on my block to see the latest film." I absolutely loved the movie. I literally laughed till I cried. It seemed much better to me than *A Hard Day's Night.* The use of comic book titles, like "A Well Known Palace" and "A Tiger" cracked me up no end, and I thought the songs were superb. I was moved by the bitterness of "You've Got to Hide Your Love Away" and the drive of "Help!" I stayed to see the film twice and was disappointed that it seemed to go so quickly the second time. I remember hearing the sound-track album at a country club party and begging my sister to buy it. "No!" she said. "If you want it, you buy it."

"But," I wailed, raising my standard objection, "I don't have anything to play it on."

1966

*. . . when the green bird of innocence had flown
and all our yesterdays seemed more important
than all our tomorrows would ever be . . .*

I remember riding with my mother one day in early 1966 to pick up my brother at grade school. While I sat in the car waiting for him to come out, shivering in the chill January air, the radio played a song by the Beatles I hadn't heard before. It had a nice melody and was decent enough, but what intrigued me most were the lyrics, which were partly sung in French. I had begun my second year of study in the language at Old Mission, and so the song, which of course was "Michelle," seemed like a special reward given to me for having to endure French class.

Rick Patrick got the *Rubber Soul* album, on which "Michelle" appeared, soon after its release in December 1965. He came over one day, wearing a brown leather jacket, his dark hair now curling over his collar, and showed me the record cover.

I was repelled. I'm sorry, but I thought that the Beatles had finally gone too far. The fisheye lens had captured their worst features and twisted them in hideous perspective. Their long hair, once merely daring, now seemed girlish, freakish. The smug look on Lennon's face and that little curl below his ear—plus the fact that his right eye is looking at you while his left is gazing somewhere far away—made me hate the man with an irrational passion. I despised Ringo's effeminate-looking hair. George's hollow-cheeked, weary expression made him look surly and a little mean. Paul was staring aloofly off camera. Even the title was printed in eerie, distorted lettering. I felt the Beatles were sticking their tongues out and saying, "We don't care about you anymore."

I realize now what it was that so turned me off. It wasn't the scruffy jackets or the outrageous hair, which now even my best friend was wearing. It wasn't the cold attitude captured by the camera. It was their faces. The Beatles looked old.

For a while they had been "one of us," youthful, vibrant, still innocent. The *Rubber Soul* sleeve penetrates that gauzy facade and shows us the effect of stress-filled tours and painful working hours. It was as though they had matured suddenly, overnight, while leaving us blindly unaware, lost in the innocuous haze of their music.

George Harrison, in a later interview, put it well: "People said, 'The problem with the Beatles is that when we were all growing up, they were all on tour and so they missed the growing-up period.' But the truth of

As 1966 rolled around, the Beatles took off in new directions, musically and personally. My hair started showing signs of Beatle influence, as can be seen in this family portrait.

(Above) Rubber Soul *was as much the product of Beatle genius as it was of George Martin, shown opposite in photos from 1962 recording sessions.*

it is that we were snatched out of our youth, or we snatched ourselves out of it. It was as though we were force-grown, like rhubarb. We went through more experiences in six years than I think most people have gone through in their lives."

And it showed. And I wanted nothing more to do with them.

It was unfortunate that the cover of *Rubber Soul* so repelled me because it prevented me from enjoying the outstanding music within. I instantly and naively banished the Beatles from my brain. It wasn't until years later that I came to appreciate the album as a strong step by the group toward artistic integrity.

No single was released from the American version of the album, although "Michelle" would have done well on its own. A duo called David and Jonathan released their own version, which was very faithful to the sound and arrangement of the original. McCartney once commented that "A lot of people said 'Michelle' would have made a good single. There are songs which we like but we wouldn't like to have out as singles. 'Cause it's a very funny thing about putting a single out. We always used to think for a single we'd have to have something pretty fast. I don't know why. They always sounded like the singles. So when we did 'Michelle,' we all thought it was okay, but we just didn't want it out as representative of us at the time."

Beatles record producer George Martin, reflecting on the structure of the album as a whole, said, "I think *Rubber Soul*, really, was the first of the Beatles' albums which presented a new Beatles to the world. Up till then we had been making albums rather like a collection of their singles. Now we were really beginning to think about albums as a bit of art on their own, as entities of their own. And *Rubber Soul* was the first to emerge in this way."

Now, with the benefit of 20/20 hindsight, I look on *Rubber Soul* as a masterpiece. I call it the Beatles' "wood and smoke" album. It generates for me a feeling of deep-colored, paneled rooms and warm fires, of wine and haze. There is a strong emphasis on acoustic instrumentation throughout, which makes me feel as if the Beatles are sitting around in my living room, unmiked and unamped, playing spontaneously and with sincerely friendly feeling. "I've Just Seen a Face" shows Paul in a happy, surprisingly witty mood. He stretches the lyric to fit his need, letting the rhymes fall in wonderfully unexpected places. The rapid guitar work matches his torrential, bouncy lyric line. Lennon lets us relax a little with the casual but intense classic, "Norwegian Wood." Again the emphasis is acoustic, but the introduction of George's now-famous sitar signals the beginning of an entirely new phase of musical culture. The song is sad, told through a major chord which suddenly shifts to a minor one. Although McCartney's bass is disappointingly inappropriate, the group takes an essentially one-chord song and keeps it from ever becoming boring. It is surprisingly brief (exactly two minutes) yet laden with a yellow regret. The last image, a fade-out on the singer alone in the room staring at the fire, is highly visual, almost cinematic.

This mood is broken and a new one created when "You Won't See Me" crashes in. It is a trebly, bursting piece, easily hummable and invitingly sing-alongable. And I could swear the thing slows down before it reaches the end. Harrison's contribution, "Think for Yourself," continues his string of darker compositions. Its cautionary, bitter tone foreshadows Lennon's angry songs on Side Two. I believe that one of George's greatest contributions to the group's sound was his bold and creative use of harmony vocals. He consistently triple- and quadruple-tracked harmonies in his own voice, creating a rich texture in each of his recordings. He learned to develop his songwriting art through contact with John and Paul; they in turn enhanced their own songs by using his style of harmony technique.

"The Word" is an eerie little song, its chorus consisting of minor chords sung over major sevenths. The jerky *boom-chick* rhythm is smoothed out by a layer of frosting from a tinny, insistent harmonium played by none other than George Martin, the Beatles' multitalented producer.

"Michelle" is a small miracle. It changes keys three times in as many bars yet never seems to wander. The tight backup vocals create a feeling of real support, almost as if the other Beatles are urging Paul on to tell his story. If they had been less careful, the Beatles might have resorted to a string section to enhance the piece, but they held to the acoustic-guitar format. It is McCartney's song all the way, as he lets his velvety bass take the solo bridge. The efforts of the singer to tell of his love to someone who can't understand his language is agonizingly complex and heartbreaking. Good job, fellas.

Side Two is really Lennon's, and it is a bittersweet delight. He is at his full literary power in "It's Only Love," where he jams the first verse with seventeen assonating or rhyming syllables. "Girl" has an almost Slavic feeling, especially in its refrain and instrumental passages. The "tit-tit" backup vocals are a subtle

schoolboy joke, but Lennon's intense sigh on an intake of breath is quite moving. Ringo steps out for his debut on keyboards in "I'm Looking Through You," a swift-moving, rocking little number. "In My Life" is one of Lennon's best, one of those really personal songs of his which like "Help!" look back to his childhood. George Martin plays a baroque keyboard embellishment that adds a touch of class to an already sincere and beautiful song. "Wait" doesn't seem to me to be quite fully realized, stopping and starting as roughly as it does.

The album ends with a decidedly wicked tone, with Lennon no longer willing to take the pain given him by the women of "Norwegian Wood" and "Girl." Instead, in "Run for Your Life," he threatens death to a girl after catching her with another man. His lyric is sharp, but there is a deadly slur to the vocal, as if sung by a drunken, thick-tongued, and angry man. It is a chilly note to finish on, but an effective one.

As good as the album seems to me now, at the time I ignored it. It seems I wasn't the only one who had wearied of the Beatles. The announcement of George's wedding on January 21, 1966, was buried on an inside page of the paper. He married Patti Boyd, the blonde schoolgirl in the dining car to whom McCartney makes his "shy" advances in *A Hard Day's Night*. Only one letter of protest was printed in the Kansas City paper, accusing Ringo of "infidelity," George of "traitorousness," and John of "disloyalty" in choosing brides. The girl who wrote the letter threatened to throw herself off a building should Paul, "our all in all," commit the same "social error."

For a while a new craze took the spotlight away from the Beatles. ABC-TV entered "Batman" on its list of midseason replacements. It was an instant smash with the critics as well as with the public. And with me. The program had a unique format: the first half was shown on Wednesday night and always ended with Batman snared in some cliff-hanging peril. The following night the story was concluded, and bat fans the country over could breathe easily. I missed the very first episode, but I insisted on getting my piano lesson over early so I could watch the Thursday installment. Mr. Rendina, the piano teacher, could sense something in the air and knew my attention was focused elsewhere.

I had a little clique of friends to whom "Batman" and "Lost in Space" were as crucial as milk on our cornflakes. We'd find each other at school before our first-hour classes and rehash the plots and puns of the night before. The shows' clichés ("Holy Iceberg, Batman!") became our own, and more than once I scratched my head over a test question, muttering to myself like the space robot, "That does not compute." In the fan columns that appeared in the TV and roto sections every Sunday, queries about Batman and Robin replaced those about the Beatles and Ringo.

While the caped crusaders battled their colorful villains, I was struggling to keep ahead of encroaching acne, the teen trauma. I was using a face cream product called "Tackle," which, as its name suggests, was

(Opposite) The artistic spark between musicians and producer created a new concept in entertainment: records (like Rubber Soul) *conceived as albums, rather than just as collections of singles.*

supposed to be a mannish way of handling the problem. It was an orangish gel with a smell like formaldehyde and a sting like Mercurochrome on an open gash. Every morning I woke up, peeled off the layer of gunk Tackle left behind and expected to see a complexion as smooth as a hazelnut. No such luck. Eventually I pitched the Tackle tube into the wastebasket and turned to the hope that time—plus occasional soap and water—heals all wounds.

I had the Beatles to blame for my complexion. According to the American Medical Association, doctors were finding more cases of skin ailments since teenagers started wearing their hair in the styles introduced by the Beatles. "Although doctors do not agree on why overhanging hair, like the over-the-forehead style recently adopted by so many boy fans of the Beatles, and the untrimmed straight hair that falls down the faces of so many young girls, aggravates many cases of acne, they do agree that there is a definite relationship," reported Linda Allen of the AMA. "Unless the teen-ager keeps his hair off his face, he may end up with what may well be termed 'Beatle skin.'"

Thanks a lot, Beatles.

Meanwhile, back at school, I was starting to emerge from my shell. I had joined the Key Club, a charity group that went about doing good deeds, and I was growing more active in scouting affairs. I started my second novel, an ambitious little opus called *Point of Calm*, based on the concept that there is a point on the earth where the winds don't blow. Verne was still my mentor, but the story began taking on a heavily sociological theme of which I was rather proud. I was still a little slow when it came to other things, however. There I was, cheering my lungs out for my favorite teacher in the student-faculty basketball game.

"You idiot!" the guy next to me shouted. "You're supposed to root for the students!"

"I thought we were supposed to yell for the teachers we liked," I protested.

"You're not supposed to like *any* of them!"

Oh, I said to myself. I was silent after that. I was totally cowed; I don't even remember who won.

One night at dinner my father asked us how we'd like to have a color television set. We practically knocked him over in our enthusiasm, and behold, the set arrived the next day. I remember frantically trying to tune in "The Man from U.N.C.L.E.," a difficult

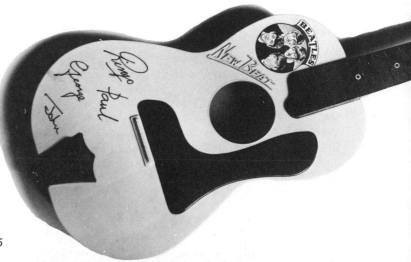

task at best since we still had no antenna. In the years that followed I wasted more hours in front of that set. I watched anything I could, from "Combat" and "The Red Skelton Hour" to "Green Acres" and "Danny Kaye." My participation in Key Club activities suffered whenever "The Avengers" was on.

I watched the Academy Awards, although I had seen very few of the movies nominated. Julie Andrews had been mentioned for *The Sound of Music*, a film my parents had taken me to that winter. I had fallen in love with her and wrote her a letter to tell her so, but she never answered. During the awards she was shown waiting backstage for the announcement of who won the Best Actress statue. She didn't win. Julie Christie did, and I was so mad I cried. I wrote *my* Julie another letter to cheer her up, but she didn't answer that one either.

Come back, Julie. All is forgiven.

The Sound of Music was the first record I remember buying. I dragged Susie's portable into my room and for about two months I played the sound track every morning before I went to school. One song, "I Have Confidence," used to run through my head on days that I had gym class. We had to run obstacle courses, and I used to climb ropes, dive over tires, and turn somersaults with the inspiring strains of Rodgers and Hammerstein urging me on to glory.

After school, while I had to pound away at the keyboard, trying to please Mr. Rendina with scales and sonatinas, Rick was learning to play guitar *and* his brother's drum set. Guitars were now the "in" thing, and everybody but me had one. The Beatles had revolutionized America's musical orientation: In 1960 a Manhattan music store sold two guitars a week; five years later it was selling sixty a day. Everyone was forming his own band—the Basement Beatles in every neighborhood were emerging into light.

In Cuba smuggled Beatles albums were selling for forty dollars apiece. A barber declared that long "Beatle hair" was out and careful styling and hair treatments for men were in. A clothing manufacturer, Mac-Gregor-Doniger, marketed "Beatle suits," featuring nipped-waist jackets with angled side vents, and lowrising, hip-hugging trousers which tapered in from the thigh to the calf, then flared at the shoe. Wide belts replaced those skinny things we'd been wearing, and boots were considered stylish. Not to be outdone, Walter Ellson, the Dior of the dog world, designed a series of leather coats for canines, which featured matching "Beatle caps." Spiffy spaniels and charming Chihuahuas may have brightened the curbs of the world, but our poodle Cozy had to be content with her original fur.

Enthusiasm for the Beatles had been whipped to a frenzy by more than two years of exposure in all of the media. As 1966 rolled on, however, that phenomenon called Beatlemania slowly evaporated, and with it went any remaining favorable feelings I had for the

In January, George married Patti Boyd, an actress he'd met while they were both working on A Hard Day's Night. *Paul was then the only one unattached; a fan's sweat shirt tells the whole story.*

group, and I began to lose interest.

As if to revive flagging enthusiasm, the TV special, "The Beatles Live at Shea Stadium," was shown that spring. The footage was from the August 15 concert of the year before and so bore little relevance to the musical progress the boys had made. The show opened with Arthur Fiedler, conductor of the Boston Pops Orchestra, giving a testimonial to the importance of the group. Documentary clips of the Beatles' arrival in New York, their trip to the stadium, and their dressing for the performance, were interspliced with scenes of the other music groups that appeared that night warming up the already feverish crowd. What a thankless task it must have been to be a preshow act for the Beatles. No one was listening, no one cared; the screams were all for the Beatles. The special was a nice little time capsule. It captured all that was bad in pop music at the time. Knee-booted go-go dancers in Cleopatra makeup frugged frenetically to saxophone-heavy music, and a combo called Sounds Unlimited, wearing the collarless suit style that the Beatles had discarded a year earlier, performed choreographed steps to their own dull sounds.

Finally the Beatles came on, and I remember lying on the couch and booing and hissing their every move. I hated the songs they played, their hair, their clothes, their obnoxious personalities. I don't know why I felt so anti-Beatle, nor why I felt I had to curse and hurl vocal abuse. But I did. Looking back, I feel rather like a fool.

I've seen the concert several times now, as part of various Beatle film festivals, and it is quite good. Lennon is a great natural clown, and he cracks George up by playing the electric piano with his elbow. Paul is charming, and while Ringo doesn't quite smash the drums the way he used to in his earlier concerts, he is a personable and effective drummer. The predictable shots of girls being carried off the field, fainting, and crying into handkerchiefs lent by bemused concession men, are marvelously funny.

The Beatles' long hot summer began with the release of "Paperback Writer" and "Rain" on May 23, 1966. Although the record eventually reached the number-one position, it did not do so immediately—the first time that had happened since "Love Me Do." It took *two* weeks for the Beatles to top the charts, during which time Frank Sinatra's "Strangers in the Night" outsold them. Of course the newspapers pounced on the comparative slowness of the song to catch on, and everyone pronounced the death of the Beatles. A promoter of the big-band sound in Las Vegas declared that "bebop has bopped and the Beatles are beaten."

A minor disaster was reported when John's father Frederick announced his intention to remarry and said that his son wasn't invited to the wedding. "John has forgotten me," he moaned. "Since he became famous, we've only met once. Of course, he'll be welcome if he wants to come." It was an indication of greater Lennon faux pas yet to come.

On June 15 Capitol released the *Yesterday and Today* album, a bastard hybrid of songs culled from the British versions of *Help!*, *Rubber Soul*, and the yet-unreleased *Revolver*. The brouhaha over this record centered on its cover, a photograph of the Beatles in butcher aprons, surrounded by cuts of meat and dismembered baby dolls with cigarette burns. The Beatles are smiling, almost maniacally. All in all, a little bizarre. Capitol quickly recalled the sleeves after one day on the stands, due to public outcry over the "lapse of taste." They pasted on a new cover, showing the Beatles in and around a steamer trunk. Hardly controversial, but the contrast is hilarious. They are no longer smiling—Paul looks as though he's about to cry—and their faces, especially Ringo's, are bathed in a seasick green tint. It's as if the boys had been beaten into submission to change the cover, so they went sullen and pouted. It's ironic, since the Beatles had nothing to do with this record. It was all the product of a Capitol records packager. Fans soon found that the old cover could be revealed by steaming off the new one. Somewhere out there are 750,000 butcher covers, worth more than a hundred dollars each to collectors.

I like *Yesterday and Today* a lot more now than I did then. Actually, I believe Capitol did us a favor by releasing the squeezings from other records in this way. They took what to my mind are some of the Beatles' worst songs and put them onto one album, as if to purify *Rubber Soul* and *Revolver*. "Drive My Car" has no business being anywhere, as far as I'm concerned. The vocal is rough and unmelodic. The harmony is discordant and harsh, and the instrumental guitar solo is unimaginative and dull. "Beep beep mm beep beep" indeed. "I'm Only Sleeping" is a little better. Its interest lies mostly in its production, with its faraway vocals and silvery arrangement. The bass notes pop up like little bubbles, nice counterpoint to the dark chords and backward guitar riff, which was to become a subject for criticism when overused in later recordings. Lennon's inclusion of a yawn in the song makes an ironic statement on a possible lack of enthusiasm either on his

The notorious "butcher" cover, censored by public outcry over its "lapse of taste," was pasted over with a more subdued photo. Albums with both covers intact sell to collectors today for $150.

part or on the part of the audience. "Nowhere Man" is pretty, wallowing as it does in thick harmonies and a beautiful solo by Harrison. The structure here is different, the solo coming far earlier than ever before in a Lennon-McCartney composition. The preachiness inherent in the lyrics is softened somewhat by the modifying "isn't he a *bit* like you and me" and the gentle "*please* listen."

"Dr. Robert" is, for me, a throwaway. It doesn't increase or decrease the Beatles' stature; it just sort of sits there. The best thing about it is the evilness that lies beneath the surface of the seemingly joyous tribute to a pillpusher. The mercury-tinged organ in the middle eight section feels like a bitter medicine in my throat, one which does little to dispel the aftertaste left by some ugly harmonies of the "Drive My Car" variety.

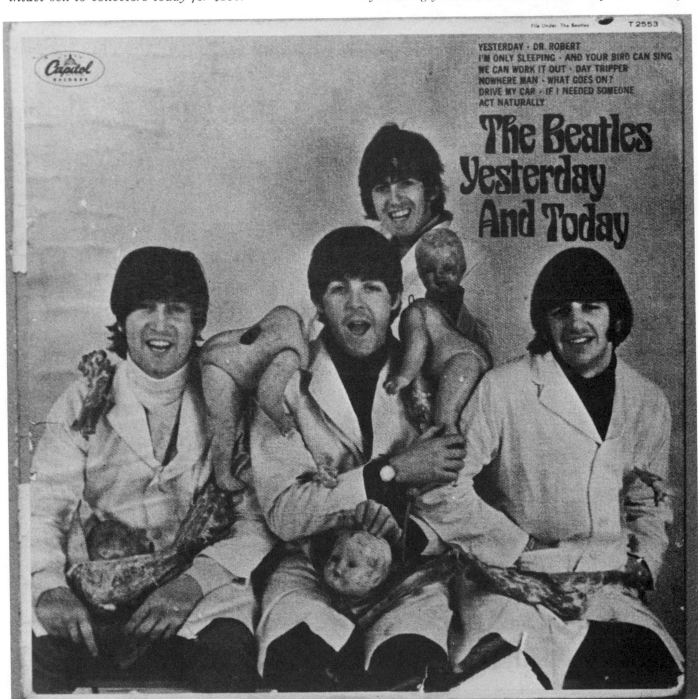

58

Now "Yesterday" is a different story. Much has been written complaining about its "fruity" string arrangement, but I think it's gorgeous. The high, teary violin sustains the whole final verse, while a sobbing cello wails underneath. It's almost self-indulgent, and I love it for that reason. Paul still plays this in some of his live appearances, and it rings in my ears whenever a past love floats into my eyes like a tear. This song, one of their biggest hits and the one most recorded by other artists, will be their most enduring.

The beauty of "Yesterday" is quickly dispelled by the clunky, clumsy "Act Naturally." It is the last song released by the Beatles that they didn't write (unless you count "Maggie Mae"), and I say good riddance. Oh, it's *okay*, but at a time when the Beatles were trying to establish themselves as studio and album artists,

it seems a greater lapse in taste than the butcher cover. But Ringo, dear, adenoidal Ringo, sings it, so that makes it all right. Besides, the lyric was prophetic. "And Your Bird Can Sing" is beautifully played and sung, but I still don't have any idea what it means. The production is muddied in the same way as "I'm Only Sleeping," but George's fluid guitar riff, which he plays with unself-conscious ease, is electrifying. The surprise shift in harmony during the third verse helps keep the song alive.

George's "If I Needed Someone" is, again, all right but nothing to shout about. The vocal is almost too insistently offbeat, and the essentially two-chord structure of the verse gets a little wearing when coupled with the droning guitar riff. The double-tracked vocal and strong sense of harmony brand the piece as a truly

59

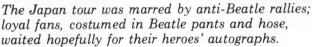

The Japan tour was marred by anti-Beatle rallies; loyal fans, costumed in Beatle pants and hose, waited hopefully for their heroes' autographs.

Harrisonish composition. "We Can Work It Out" is a beauty, carrying on the two-chord verse structure of Harrison's number. The harmonium contributes a haunting smoothness, while McCartney's reserved, rational lyric is wonderfully expressed in his assuring, mellow vocal. The ends of lines during the middle eight suddenly shift, not so much into a waltz tempo, as into a tripleted 4/4 measure. For one brief measure, during the words "fussing and," *both* time signatures are stacked against each other. The song works smoothly, due largely to the well-blended voices of John and Paul and to the lucid rhythm of their instrumentation.

"What Goes On" is the only three-way Beatle composition ever, but, like "Act Naturally," it bears little resemblance to great music. The predictable harmonies muddy up the already dull melody, and the thwacking lead guitar is only annoying. "Day Tripper," together with "We Can Work It Out" and "Yesterday," saves the album. It is a mature, exciting composition, complex and driving. McCartney's vocal is no longer gently compromising, as in "We Can Work It Out." That opening riff, or "hook" as it is condescendingly called nowadays, is well handled by George, punctuated by Paul on bass and Ringo's sizzling percussion. Each verse is slightly different in emphasis and melody, which keeps the song fresh and surprising right through to the end, where Ringo deals us a series of triplets to carry us out of the song. A job well done and one of the best and most representative of all Beatle songs. The Fab Four did a fine job of parodying themselves in this number during a videotape appearance on "Shindig."

The Beatles left for a brief tour of the Far East in June, but controversy followed them everywhere. They were threatened with death if they followed through with plans to play in Tokyo's sacred Budo Kan hall. Despite violent Bushidokan demonstrations the Beatles played the concert without incident. In Manila a refusal to attend a garden party hosted by the president of the Philippines and his wife was taken as a snub, and the Beatles found themselves in danger—not from fans, but from police, who managed to land a few punches in a few Beatle stomachs before the boys could board a plane to safety.

But the biggest public relations crisis of the Beatles' career came in early August 1966. An American teen magazine, *Datebook*, took a quotation John had made to Maureen Cleave, a reporter for the *London Evening Standard*, and printed it out of context. John had said, "Christianity will go. It will vanish and shrink. I needn't argue about that; I'm right and I will be proved right. We [the Beatles] are more popular than Jesus now; I don't know which will go first, rock 'n' roll or Christianity. Jesus was all right, but his disciples were thick and ordinary. It's them twisting it ruins it for me."

Hell hath no fury like the Bible Belt scorned. The reaction to Lennon's supposedly blasphemous statement started in Birmingham, Alabama, where radio station WAQY's manager, Tommy Charles, organized a Ban the Beatles campaign a week or so before the Beatles' tour of America was to get under way. "We just felt it [the statement] was so absurd and sacrilegious that something ought to be done to show them they cannot get away with this sort of thing," Charles said.

Yeah, boy. Go get them Beatles.

Well, the movement caught on. South Carolina and Texas were the next to jump aboard and capture a few headlines on a few back pages. The Ku Klux Klan made ominous anti-Beatle threats. In St. Louis, where

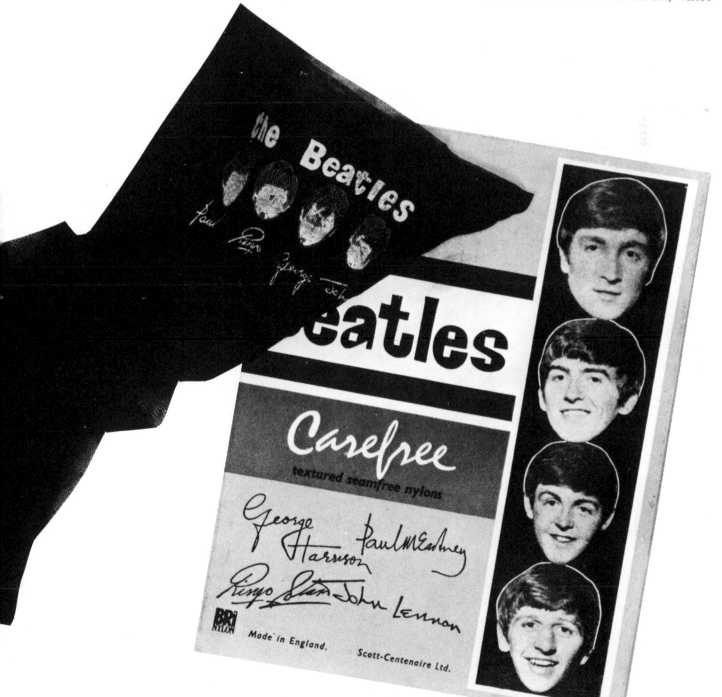

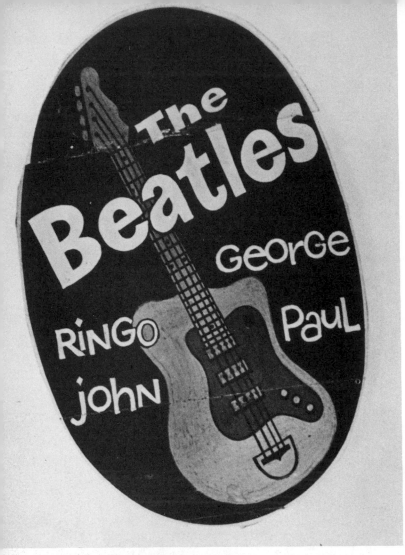

The Beatles' days of innocence were ending; John's statement, "we are more popular than Jesus now," angered fans and disc jockeys, prompting small-scale riots and record-burning sprees (opposite).

bonfires were staged at which Beatle records and souvenirs were destroyed, barefoot girls in shorts carried banners reading "We Don't Need Them." Back in Birmingham a news story ran on television with the announcement, "Our fantastic Beatle Boycott is still in effect. Don't you forget what the Beatles have said. Don't forget to take your Beatle records and your Beatle paraphernalia to any one of our fourteen pickup points in Birmingham, Alabama." Shades of Nazi Germany. I remember looking at newspaper photos which showed young kids, not old enough to think for themselves, grinning as records and books burned away to ashes.

Efforts were made by the Beatle organization to save the upcoming tour, which was already suffering at the box office. Walter Shenson, producer of *Help!* and *A Hard Day's Night*, said the ban would have no effect on his plans to star the group in a third film. "I think their loyal fans are going to remain loyal. Very loyal. And the Beatles are loyal. They are terribly decent boys when you get to know them. They have a high standard of morality." His announcement sounded as if it were made a little out of desperation.

Maureen Cleave tried to smooth things over by say-

ing that John "was certainly not comparing the Beatles to Christ. He was simply observing that so weak was the state of Christianity that the Beatles were, to many people, better known. He was deploring rather than approving this. Sections of the American public seem to have been given an impression of his views that is totally absurd." In Spain a radio station demanded the withdrawal of Lennon's statement. The only broadcast medium in Johannesburg banned Beatle records, saying the South African Broadcasting corporation "will not lend its services to fostering the image of the group in this country." Hong Kong, however, realized that "any religious belief has nothing to do with an artist's performance and the Beatles as artists," and continued to play their songs.

Meanwhile Brian Epstein, sick with glandular fever, left his bed to fly to America to gauge the extent of anti-Beatle sentiment. In a press conference in New York he said, "The quote which John Lennon made to a London columnist nearly three months ago has been quoted and misrepresented entirely out of the context of an article which was in fact highly complimentary to Lennon as a person, and was understood by him to be exclusive to the *Evening Standard*. It was not anticipated that it would be displayed out of context and in such a manner as it was in an American teenage magazine."

A minister in Kansas City sided with Lennon, saying, "The Beatle's remark is perhaps accurate, because Jesus is often misunderstood. If we really understood Jesus Christ and his message He would be the most popular man in the history of mankind." Even the Vatican newspaper got into the act, defending Lennon by saying that his remark was made "offhandedly and not impiously. He spoke without thinking about the importance of his words on Christ and religion," but "this is a sign that some subjects must not be dealt with lightly, in a profane way, even in the world of beatniks."

The Beatles, bless their hearts, did not know when to let bad enough alone. While Epstein was trying to quell the revolts, the Beatles' press office issued a statement that Lennon was deeply interested in religion and had meant "that in the last fifty years the church in England and therefore Christ had suffered decline in interest. He did not mean to boast about the Beatles' fame." McCartney was elsewhere, telling David Frost that he liked America but not as much as England because the people of the United States "seem to believe that money is everything. . . . You get the feeling everybody's after it—money—and it's sort of frightening." Meanwhile Harrison discussed the upcoming U.S. trip, saying, "I'm not looking forward to it, except for California, which comes at the end of the tour. There, at least, we can swim and get a bite to eat."

Letters in the *Kansas City Star* were pretty evenly divided between disillusioned fans and die-hard supporters. One letter put it simply and tolerantly, "Forgive and forget." The paper even ran an editorial, reassuring the public that Christianity has survived more powerful assaults than Lennon's. It would be difficult for the Beatles to sing, it added, with Lennon's foot in four mouths.

On August 11 the Beatles arrived in Chicago and faced a crowd of hostile newsmen, unsatisfied with the denials and explanations. In Kansas City, I remember, we had been playing in the streets, under the warm shower of light from a streetlamp, surrounded by the busy-signal buzz of a million cicadas. Susie ran out of the house yelling that Lennon was going to "take it back." Good, I thought. Put that man in his place. Besides no longer liking the Beatles I was now angry with them, and I was glad they were finally being taken down a few notches. We stood on the front porch, listening to the radio in hushed silence with a group of neighborhood kids, waiting for the announcement of Lennon's retraction.

The disc jockeys played up the press conference as the biggest thing since Pompeii. It was as though we were all standing around a beaten man, waiting for him to cry uncle so we could laugh in smug superiority. I don't remember if the conference was carried live, but I do remember the elation and the triumph we felt when Lennon swallowed his pride, his ego, and his words in one universal gulp.

Tony Barrow, a press officer for NEMS (the name of Epstein's company in Liverpool which became the Beatles organization), remembered how the conference went. "John was more frightened, really scared stiff that night, than I've ever seen him, because the whole thing fell on his shoulders. It wasn't a Beatles' press conference, with a few nifty wisecracks and passing the joke to and fro. This was John on his own, coming out into the hotel room filled with journalists and cameramen and so forth, and unfortunately the reporters there still seemed to have gotten the wrong impression. John went to great lengths; he spent perhaps five or ten minutes trying to explain what he had *not* meant as well as what he *had* meant. He wasn't boasting that night in the hotel. He personally faced the press in his own right, not particularly as a Beatle. He took a great personal responsibility and was greatly concerned lest this thing should be taken out of context. He didn't blame Maureen Cleave in the least, because the way he'd said it to her had been reported the way he'd said it. But he was very concerned that the whole thing could rebound on the Beatles."

John, nervous and subdued, looking very small, faced the press and said, "If I'd have said television was more popular than Jesus, I might have got away with it. As I just happened to be talking with a friend I used the word Beatles as a remote thing, not as what I think—as Beatles, as those other Beatles like other

(Above) Brian Epstein tried to quell anti-Beatle anger on the eve of their final American tour; John swallowed his misunderstood words at a press conference which made front-page news (opposite). "I'm sorry I said it, really," he said. "I never meant it as a lousy antireligious thing."

people see us. And I just said 'they' as having more influence on kids and things than anything else, including Jesus. But I said it in that way, which is the wrong way. But I'm not saying that we're better or greater or comparing us with Jesus Christ as a person, or God as a thing, or whatever it is. I just said what I said and it was wrong, or it was taken wrong, and now there's all this."

Tony Barrow again: "And at the end of this great long, fairly humble explanation, up popped a reporter and said, 'Okay, but the main point is, John, are you prepared to apologize,' meaning in other words that they just hadn't taken the point of this at all. And in desperation at the end of that session, I remember John saying, 'Okay, well, look, you know, if that will make you all happy, I'll apologize. I still don't know quite what I've done, I've tried to tell you what I did do, but if you want me to apologize, if that'll make you happy, I will do.'"

The next day, front page center, appeared the headline, "Beatle Apologizes for Remark." "I'm sorry, I'm sorry I said it really," John lamented in the article. "I never meant it as a lousy, antireligious thing."

The Beatles were no longer infallible. We had dug and dug to find some breach in their personalities, to find some fault to magnify and gloat over. Well, we did it. After the years of constant exposure to the public, a verbal fistfight had erupted, and the Beatles were the losers.

No one can blame them for ending all public appearances at the conclusion of the U.S. tour. (Ironically, the Memphis concert on August 19, which city officials had threatened with cancellation because of John's remark, was attended by thirty thousand fans, three times the number attending a rally for Jesus held in the same city that night.) The Beatles' last concert appearance was at Candlestick Park in San Francisco on August 29, 1966. Tony Barrow remembers: "Coming out of San Francisco that night, getting aboard the charter flight to fly back down the west coast of California to L.A., one of the first things George Harrison said when he leaned back in the plane and took a drink was, 'Well, that's it. I'm finished. I'm not a Beatle anymore'. "

Brian Epstein sensed the end of touring had come and with it the end of his real responsibilities to the Beatles. His prime function had been to manage the tours; he had had little to do with them artistically. Now it seemed to him that he would no longer be needed. This sense of loss probably contributed to his death late in 1967.

Speaking of concerts, George said, "The sound was always bad and we'd just be joking to each other to keep ourselves amused. It was very impersonal. And not only that. There were so many police and kids flying around. It was really like we'd got into a big political thing with all that Christ thing, and at that time I was just so sick of it. I think we all were. We were just like nervous wrecks. Getting flown around everywhere . . . press conferences everywhere we went . . . just too much."

As if to give themselves a breather, from the public as well as from each other, the Beatles took separate holidays that fall and pursued their own interests. John cut his hair to a 1914 style for his role in Richard Lester's *How I Won the War*, while Paul went off to write background music for *The Family Way*. The themes of his music on that album are quite pleasant. One features a baroque-influenced brass section and contemporary percussion; another is a beautifully melancholy piece with flute and guitar. The album, though enhanced by George Martin's arrangements and orchestrations, is a little dull, since its unnamed tracks are just variations on the same two themes. It is a less-than-successful effort, and McCartney knew it.

At the end of 1966 the Beatles had taken a bold step in their development as artists. They quit touring and committed themselves to studio work. More important, however, was their experimentation with the effects of marijuana and LSD. Their music had already taken on elements of drug-oriented surrealism, subtly so in *Rubber Soul* and more conspicuously so in "Rain." *Revolver*, released August 8, took them even further into the weird world of psychedelia. One song from that album, "Eleanor Rigby," was to win me back to the numbers of their fans. The Beatles had changed the world once. They were about to do it again.

Beatle Apologizes for Remar

The faithful in England weep as the Beatles leave

The Beatles wave good-by to their fans

Chicago fans give singers same old welcome

CHICAGO (AP)—Beatle John Lennon apologized last night for a widely publicized remark that "the Beatles are more popular than Jesus."

"I'm sorry, I'm sorry I said it really. I never meant it as a lousy, anti-religious thing,"

he told a news conference at which the quartet was bombarded with questions about Lennon's remarks on Christianity.

"I was sort of deploring the attitude toward Christianity," he replied. "I wasn't saying the Beatles are better than

God or Jesus. I use "'Beatles' because it's ea for me to talk about Beatles. could have said TV or th cinema or anything popular

He continued: "At first was just one of those thing

(Continued on Page 2.)

Strike MORE CHINESE

65

1967

. . . when all the lonely-hearted people sang along with just a little help from their friends and through the flowers of cellophane we saw a world that turned us on . . .

The Beatles and I had had a quarrel, but it turned out to be merely a separation, not a divorce. When they released *Revolver* and its corresponding single "Eleanor Rigby"/"Yellow Submarine" in August 1966, I was still not ready to admit them back to my world, but I was at least willing to listen more carefully.

By now Rick and I, sadly, were going our separate ways. I began to think of him as "older" than I. He would duck under a little bridge near his house and sneak a quick cigarette, an act which I found frighteningly daring. His other friends and I didn't get along very well, and he began spending more time with them. I had always thought that fashions were something only people in the newspapers followed, but Rick was sporting long hair and the latest shirts while I limped along in my modest, fading styles. My new best friend, James, was a more conservative guy who shared my interests in science fiction and scouting. I had dropped out of my old troop and joined a new one, and I persuaded James to come along.

I remember that Rick had a pair of sunglasses that were really "mod." They were metal-framed, with square lenses. When I saw the cover of *Revolver* I knew why he wore them. On the back of the jacket is a picture of the Beatles looking just too cool in wild print shirts and far-out shades. Rick, who bore a striking resemblance to Lennon anyway, was now going a step further—a step too far, I thought.

The front of the *Revolver* jacket is always described by critics as "austere." Perhaps it is a little somber, but it is by no means simple. This is the first of their record sleeves by an artist other than Robert Freeman, who had been their photographer from the very first. *Revolver* was designed by bass guitarist Klaus Voorman (if you look carefully you can see his face, popping out from between strands of George's hair) who was later to strike up a musical association with the Beatles as solo artists. Many of the photographs on the cover are, ironically, ones Freeman included in his concert souvenir programs. Real pictures of Beatle eyes are spliced onto line drawings of Beatle faces, creating a weird, staring effect. The "drawn" John is mischievously eyeing the "live" photographs, some of which date back to the Beatles' first recording sessions.

The music of *Revolver*, like the cover, emphasizes how far the Beatles had come since "Love Me Do." Its first track, "Taxman," opens with the first snippet of "accidental" studio noise heard on a Beatle record. Throats are cleared, an incredibly deep-sounding George gives a menacing "one-two-three-four" downbeat while guitars are tuned and someone shouts "go" in the background. To me this signals that the group had entered the studio, once and for always, never again to emerge except as individuals.

"Taxman," one of three Harrison compositions on the record, is generally regarded to be his finest, although I prefer some of his later "White Album" cuts. In keeping with the sinister tone of the song, the chord

1967, the year the Beatles were reborn as Sgt. Pepper and his band (opposite), was the year I turned 15 and rediscovered the group.

Revolver's cover (above) prefigured the elaborate (and expensive) psychedelia of the Sgt. Pepper sleeve, for which the Beatles sprouted bushy, trend-setting mustaches (opposite).

George plays twice after each line of the verse is ugly and dissonant. Paul's bass is marvelous—listen to its precision in maintaining the rhythmical submelody. The lyrics are biting and sharp and show Harrison at his ironic best. I love it when the little chorus comes in, clucking its tongue and shaking its finger, saying "ah, ah, Mr. Wilson, ah, ah, Mr. Heath." You naughty boys, you. A furious Indian-flavored solo on electric guitar emerges during the song and again at the end, increasing the raw intensity of the piece.

This is the first Beatle song that is in any way tinged with a political color. Until now the Beatles had justly (and wisely) steered away from any controversy in their music, although their actions and personalities caused numberless staid hackles to rise. "Taxman" also reveals George's reputed obsession with money and materialism. Throughout their career, until Epstein's death, George was the only one who ever challenged his manager on contract matters and was supposedly always the one most worried about going broke. When asked in a press conference in Kansas City whether they preferred the Labour party or the Conservative, George replied, "We'll vote for the one that will cut taxes the most." "Taxman" seems like a rather stern slap at both parties, an honest if ungracious reply to the government that had honored them with MBEs. George's dedication to materialism was soon to change, of course, under the influence of Eastern philosophy.

The second song on Revolver is "Eleanor Rigby," which I think is one of the three best songs the Beatles have done. It's ironic that only one Beatle voice appears on the record (Paul's), although George did have an uncredited hand in writing the lyrics. No Beatle instruments are heard, their guitars having been traded in on a magnificent baroque string quartet. The only Beatle record to win a Grammy award as best song of the year, "Eleanor Rigby" shows the continuing emergence of Paul as an individual artist and hints at the further splintering within the group structure that was to produce some of their best (and their worst) music. The strength of the song lies in the overpowering loneliness of the lyric, heightened by the emotional yet coldly distant string arrangement. Paul begins here his technique of telling a story in the third person, a trick that works beautifully to isolate and objectify the depressingly desperate chasm of Eleanor's loneliness. In a triumph of recording wizardry, the chorus sings "look at all the *lovely* people" while the lead sings "*lonely* people." At one point I think he may even be saying "lowly." Each subtle switch of sound piles another depth of meaning onto an already annihilating song.

"Love You To" is the first Beatle piece to feature strictly Indian instrumentation, although the sitar had its Western pop debut in *Rubber Soul*. The beginning, a dreamy raga-style improvisation, gives way suddenly to the singularly awkward and bitter lyric. The tempo speeds up once again at the end, furiously racing into a fade-out. (There are rumors that about this time George recorded an album for Capitol under the pseudonym of "Lord Sitar," which included such unlikely cuts as the Stones' "Have You Seen Your Mother Baby Standing in the Shadows." Nowadays copies of the record are sold as Beatle collector's items, but I have never heard any confirmation from the Beatles or from any Beatle literature that George did in fact record it, nor do I believe frankly that he was ever good enough on sitar to attempt such a project. In his only public appearance with a sitar, on the "Dick Cavett Show" years later, he admitted he was pretty bad at the instrument and when asked to play, could barely get through a painfully executed C-major scale.)

Paul shines again with the very tender "Here There and Everywhere." Musically the piece is a little weak, its melody running through a string of bland ascending chords. A nice twist comes when the singer says she changes his life "with a wave of her hand," and just at that moment the song changes key, as if her "wave" was felt even during the recording. Paul's vocal is innocent, almost to the point of being cloying, but his wide-eyed gentleness gives me a sense that his love is pure and purifying. I don't like George's twangy guitar chords, which seem like rude interruptions to a very intimate conversation.

And then there's "Yellow Submarine." John wrote this because he liked the idea of little kids walking around singing it. I think it's charming, and I remember feeling that the Beatles—or John alone— should make a record of original children's songs. If you listen closely, you can hear a bubbling noise under much of the song, as well as the multitalented Lennon acting as the entire submarine crew, from steersman to captain ("Lock the chambers! Lock the chambers!"). The final incantations of "We all live in a yellow submarine" sound like a thousand-voice choir singing away inside the sub.

"She Said She Said" had its origins in the Beatles' encounters with LSD. They had first been slipped some in their coffee by a friend; later they tried it on their own. This particular trip taken at a party resulted in a confusing conversation of the "I said that you said that she said I said" variety. Drugs, at least in this instance, didn't seem to help the Beatles to find a clearer image of themselves.

"Good Day Sunshine" is a nifty little ditty. The opening piano chords hold our interest through Ringo's cymbal crash, which seems to herald the sun's arrival, as does the sudden change of key. The recording, especially of the piano, is a little murky, but Paul's clear vocal brings the song back into focus. There is a country-boy naïveté about the good-time spirit, which contrasts well with Simon and Garfunkle's "city" songs of a similar nature. Paul does well with the rhythm of the piece, which is consistently 4/4 time throughout but which, through shifts of word stress and offbeat percussion, sounds infinitely more complicated.

"For No One" is an achingly beautiful piece. It is the emotional flip side of "Here There and Everywhere," expressing through a flawless lyric the many ways loneliness is felt. McCartney tries to take a neutral stand between "she" and "you," but the passion in his voice belies his true feelings. The poetry of the words is stunning. The day breaks, and your mind aches instantly—there is no relief found even in daylight. "She no longer needs you," the song says; "you think she needs you."

How crushing those words are! "You stay home, she goes out": the picture of pain is painted in six short words. There is no sign in her eyes of the love that should have lasted years—a beautifully concise image of the death of love. The horn solo, by virtuoso Alan Civil, is a sob in the dark, which repeats itself in harmonious counterpoint to the melody line. This song still plays in my head and stings the insides of my eyes whenever I feel the sadness of lost or unrequited love.

"I Want to Tell You," the third and least impressive of George's contributions, opens with a "Day Tripper"-like riff, then drives ahead, its momentum sustained by Ringo's steady beat and Paul's one-note-per-beat bass. There seems to be a mistake in the piano part which produces an irksome discord, but since it is repeated sixty-four times in the song, we can assume it was meant to be. George plays tricks with our ears: He makes us think he has dropped two beats out of a line, but he really hasn't. The chant at the end, in customary triple-tracked harmony, shows the increasing control Harrison has over his voice.

The last Paul song on the record, "Got to Get You into My Life," shows the rockin' side of the ballad weaver. His rubbery lyric line is well rounded out by

the insistent, blaring horns. It sounds as though all the musicians are running at maximum pace, charging the song with strength and energy. The whining final trumpet note segues neatly into the exotic droning opening of "Tomorrow Never Knows," John's miasmic coda to *Revolver*. The production is the star here: Lennon's voice is all but lost in the sounds of feedback, flocks of laughing birds, and insistent percussion. Sounds float in and out, as though heard in a half-sleep. Distortions of time and motion are felt through the use of sped-up and reversed tape loops. In the third verse John sounds as though he is singing to us through a telephone or from a radio on a distant planet: His voice is distant, tinny, isolated. I always thought the "end of the beginning" refrain was prophetic, since this album certainly was the end of the first half of the Beatle's career and, as they said in *A Hard Day's Night*, "an early clue to the new direction."

After the Beatles quit touring, they had more time to dedicate to their wives and families. They saw less and less of Brian Epstein, with whom contact was mostly of a business nature. They invested in new homes in London. Paul found himself in need of a new chauffeur and a housekeeper after his old ones quit, wishing they could work for someone with "more regular hours." He advertised for replacements under the name of "Mr. Brown." Ringo was similarly hassled, plagued by what he thought was an "excessive" gardener's bill of $22,400. Ah, the trials and tribulations of domesticity.

Paul helped inaugurate the beginning of the "psychedelic" era in January 1967 by sporting a newly grown mustache. "It's part of breaking up the Beatles," he said. "I no longer believe in the image." He said he was thinking about starting a new career, that the Beatles will "work together only if we miss each other. Then it'll be hobby work. It's good for us to go it alone." This was two weeks before the Beatles signed a contract to make records as a group for nine more years. Breaking up is hard to do.

The *Kansas City Star* printed a photo of the Beatles with their new facial fur. I thought they looked rather dashing, and I felt my top lip, ruefully noting its smoothness. Shaving was something I should have done more than I did, but I hated dragging that infernal machine over my cheeks and the feeling that the "li'l tiny hairs" were being pulled out by the roots.

The Beatles released "Penny Lane" and "Strawberry Fields Forever" on February 13. Although both songs were given equal emphasis by Capitol—no real A Side was indicated, but the catalog number for "Strawberry Fields" is lower—it was "Penny Lane" that got the air play in Kansas City.

And that was fine with me. I absolutely adored the song. I thought it was supposed to be a totally surrealistic description of an Anglicized Valhalla, peopled by characters who wore bright colors and who walked to the rhythms of baroque trumpets. Despite the apparent "straightness" of the melody and arrangement I thought the Beatles had reached a new level of expression, one which spoke loudly to me. I had looked again toward the Beatles when they released "Eleanor Rigby"; now I had completely forgiven their past transgressions and entered the fold once again as an interested, if not overwhelmed, fan. It wasn't until two

years later, when I actually visited Penny Lane in Liverpool, that I was struck by the literalness of the song.

"Strawberry Fields," though touted by the critics as a great song, leaves me cold. I think the lyrics are ambling and hastily written, especially the second verse where Lennon sings "That is I think it's not too bad." The words don't scan, they don't fit, the emphasis is wrong, and they don't even *rhyme*, for Pete's sake. My main objection to the piece is the effect, which everyone else seems to find so remarkable, that there are two completely different songs being wedged together. According to George Martin they recorded two completely different versions; he sped one up and slowed the other down and somehow managed to cut them as one record.

I still don't care for it. It is slow to the point of being lethargic; it doesn't even sound like Lennon singing. The multiple fade-out, fade-in endings seem like a cliché, even for 1967. The lyrics are replete with phrases like "I mean," "that is," "I think," "you know." It's poorly written, annoyingly ambiguous, and, for me, a disappointment coming from the normally highly articulate Lennon. Amen.

By now the Beatles had transcended pop music and were nestled comfortably in every level of Western civilization. A Jesuit priest even suggested that music with a beat "in the style we may associate with the Beatles" would be "in line with church thinking for use at sacred rites." It seems that, after all the dust had settled, John's Jesus remarks had been forgotten, and the Beatles' music, their real contribution, was remembered, although I never actually heard *my* church go so far as to quote a Beatle song in a sermon.

In England John and Paul were given the Ivor Novello award for the most-performed song of 1966—"Michelle" —and as their own runners-up for "Yesterday." "Yellow Submarine" was honored as the best-selling record in Britain, 1966. In America, as mentioned earlier, they were given a Grammy for "Eleanor Rigby," the best song of the year. I applauded.

Meanwhile in London avant-garde artists staged a "14-Hour Dream," a marathon of music, lighting effects, Warhol films, and creative happenings. One such artist's happening was "a composition in music of the mind," in which a model stood before five thousand people and let volunteers snip away pieces of her clothes until she stood stark naked, surrounded by a pile of tattered cloth.

The artist's name?

Yoko Ono.

Summer came and with it the end of my junior-high career. It ended with a flourish—I wrote and directed a ten-minute sketch for our talent show commenting on Cassius Clay's refusal to be drafted. The scene, complete with three songs, featured Ernie Terrell as Cassius/Mohammad's drill sergeant in Vietnam ("Hello, Cassius, this is Ernie, Cassius, it's so nice to have you here in Vietnam . . ."). Now, however, I was faced with the bleak prospect of entering (gulp) high school. My sister showed me around the halls and classrooms, but I felt scared and out of place. I still got my kicks watching the Beatles cartoon show on Saturday mornings and the Monkees on Monday nights. My friends and I were watching such shows as "Star Trek" and

"The Time Tunnel," and I had gotten a bang out of the movie version of *Fantastic Voyage*. Ray Bradbury's *Fahrenheit 451*, the first contemporary sci-fi book I read, was released as a film, to which I happily made the required pilgrimage.

I was still struggling along musically. Our piano teacher had suffered long enough the competition with Batman in the living room. One night, after I had given a particularly disastrous performance, he slammed my hands on the keys for the last time, lifted his bulk from the chair, put on his old-man's hat, and muttered, in his Italian accent, "I quit. Too much Beatle influence."

He walked out of the room and slammed the door. We never saw him again.

I sat for a while in stunned silence. *Beatle* influence? I didn't even really *like* the Beatles—then, anyway. I didn't know whether to feel miserable and ashamed or to run down the street clicking my heels that he'd gone.

Beatle influence? Batman, maybe. But Beatles?

Mr. Rendina's farewell speech was prophetic but not immediately applicable. I wasn't quite ready to count myself among the numbers of die-hard Beatle fans. After Mr. Rendina left, my sister and I started taking lessons from Pete Eye, an extremely talented Kansas City jazz pianist, who taught me chords, a little improvisation, and an appreciation of popular music.

That summer my sister went with my mother for a three-week trip through Europe. She returned with a copy of the number-one album in England. It bore the strange title of *Sgt. Pepper's Lonely Hearts Club Band.*

I remember so clearly the first time I heard it. Every so often something happens to you that, somehow, you just *know* you're going to want to remember. John Glenn's space flight was one such event. The first play of *Sgt. Pepper* was another.

It was the middle of a Kansas summer—hot, humid, miserable; the house was vainly being cooled by an overworked, window-unit air conditioner. Susie put the record on, and as I heard the sounds of a crowd that

(Opposite top) The Beatles' wild print shirts, high collars, and wide woven belts derived from, and in turn influenced, swinging London's fashion-conscious Carnaby Street (below). (Opposite bottom) Clip from "Strawberry Fields" promo film.

(Above) Carnaby street before Beatle influence took over; note the "mod" styles. (Opposite) The Beatles as they appeared when the film Yellow Submarine went into production.

open Side One, I asked her, "Did they do this in front of an audience?"

"Ssh. Just listen," she said.

I sshed. And I listened.

The effect was magical. The songs were poetic, mystical; they emerged from a self-contained world of bizarre carnival colors; they spoke in a language and a musical idiom all their own. I was particularly struck by the mind-bending sitar on "Within You Without You" and the cheery music hall clarinets of "When I'm Sixty-four." "A Day in the Life" took my breath away, as it does today; I remember the feeling of my heart skipping a beat at that melancholy, endless final chord. I remember my eyes grew wide with delight. I played the record over and over again that day. I felt as though I'd discovered the tenth planet.

Over the years I've played *Sgt. Pepper* more than any other of my albums. Although I don't think it's the Beatles' best, it is a miraculous, overwhelming achievement. A friend I met later in England called it "the most technically perfect record ever made." That sounds vaguely like faint praise, though, for an album to whose release date, June 2, we can trace the beginning of the history of a new generation.

The cover is a confusing mélange of color and black and white, of past and present, of East and West. Even the Rolling Stones ("Good Guys") get into the act, their name written on the shirt of the doll at the far right. Everybody from Lawrence of Arabia to Edgar Allan Poe has a hand in somewhere. *Sgt. Pepper* was

the first Beatles album to print the lyrics to the songs, as if new stress were finally being put on what was being said as well as what was being played.

Sgt. Pepper emerged from the myth of "swinging London," from the shops of Carnaby Street where "uniforms, any uniforms" were all the rage. Some critics see the album retrospectively as a dated fossil, as a relic to be shelved forever along with beaded headbands, peace decals, and "flower power" bumper stickers. To do so is to overlook a triumph of recorded musical art.

The opening song emerges from the apprehensive din of tuning violins and a buzzing crowd. Without warning the drum sounds the alarm, and the guitar fanfare makes us settle in our seats for what promises to be a splendid time. The lead singer introduces us to a new/old act, Sgt. Pepper's band, that woos us with its charm ("we'd love to take you home") and its comic antics (the crowd laughs at some invisible joke). We know we're listening to the Beatles, but somehow they have transcended even themselves to create yet a new myth. Their outrageous uniforms and mustaches recall a turn-of-the-century marching band, but the sound is ultramodern. They have indeed gone in and out of style, but they're back now, on top of it all. It's as if the Beatles themselves knew they were launching an era and so chose to show it in by reintroducing themselves in their new incarnation.

Even Ringo, whose thick, off-key voice could be recognized through a thousand voice filters, is presented as a remote someone named Billy Shears. His solo, "With a Little Help from My Friends," starts with a segue from the title song and a nearly buried fanfare of "Billll—eeee—SHEARS!" (One poor befuddled essayist thought it was the Beatles saying "cheese," which sent him into throes of euphoria over the band's "amusing clowning"). Ringo sings better here than he ever had before; his vocal is relaxed and assured and his drumming more aggressively creative than most of his previous work. The question/response structure is not religiously maintained; sometimes Ringo asks his own questions ("How do I feel . . ."), sometimes he gives answers ("Yes I'm certain . . .," "I can't tell you . . ."). The constant skip-along rhythm is beautifully maintained with the help of an occasional piano track. The only real flaw in the song comes in the rough transition between the final "somebody to love" and the reprise of "Oh I get by . . ." The little trio of vocalists in the background lend beautiful support to Ringo's shining hour.

I remember that when I had my wisdom teeth out and was flat on my back in bed, some friends called to ask if they could come over. Of course, I told them. It turns out that they had been rehearsing "With a Little Help" all day on their recorders, and they wanted to give me a little concert. I smiled so broadly my mouth started bleeding again.

"Lucy in the Sky with Diamonds" won notoriety from its ostensible proximity to an LSD trip, and the coincidental initials of its title. (Actually the initials are LITSWD, which must be a drug as yet undiscovered.) John humorously attempted to explain the origin of the song in an interview. To the accompaniment of a tinkly harpsichord a narrator said, in a high, whiny Goody Gumdrop voice:

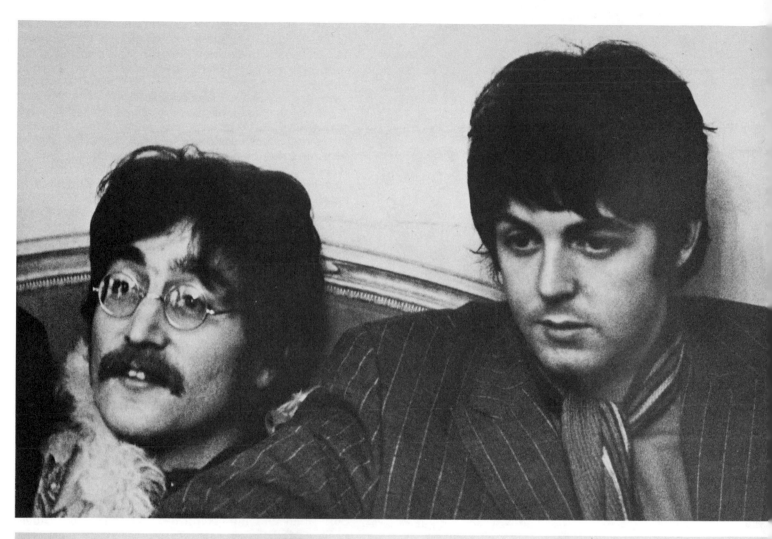

Brian Epstein objected to Sgt. Pepper's cover concept; permissions to print photos of the famous made it the costliest album sleeve ever.

"Are you sitting comfortably? Then I'll begin. One day, months ago, Julian, son of Lennon, came home from school with a painting he'd just drawn, a picture of a lady bursting with colors. John Lennon said, 'What's that you got there, Junior?' To which Junior replied, 'It's Lucy in the Sky with Diamonds, Daddy.' 'Shaddup.' [Smack!] 'Waaahhhh . . .!' "

But that didn't satisfy the wise ones of our generation. Oh no, wink wink, nudge nudge, *they* knew what he meant all along, snicker snicker. But there is no reason to doubt Lennon's official explanation. The man has always been open and honest, if not always careful, in what he says. He admitted to using drugs, he admitted to taking over a hundred LSD trips. Why on earth would he bother to deny one little story about the origins of a song unless it wasn't true?

The song itself is Lennon's most indulgent exercise in poetic imagery. I think it's wonderful that the arrangement is so sparse: For a while there is just the bass on one track and a guitar or keyboard of some kind on the other, with John's three-tone vocal emerging from the middle somewhere. This dryness serves to highlight the language, which shines with a crystalline gleam. The words are "Plasticine," "kaleidoscope," "marshmallow," "tangerine," and "marmalade," each a polysyllabic encapsulation of a bright or glittering object. The dreamlike vocal is enhanced by a waltz tempo and delicate cymbal riffs. Further austerity comes when the lead guitar, instead of harmonizing, follows the vocal melody line. Everything is tight, precise, controlled. Then suddenly the jewellike atmosphere is shattered by three explosive drumbeats, after which the song shifts to a 4/4 time for the "Lucy in the sky" refrain. There seem to be two songs spliced together, as in "Strawberry Fields," but more cohesively joined.

I love the song, especially the beautifully strong chorus and the chord change on the sustained "Ah-hh—h . . ." I played the record for a friend of the family, an older man, to impress him with the beauty of contemporary music. He said it sounded like an Arabian shepherd sitting on a sand dune and whining for his sheep to come home. I was miffed.

I'm not too fond of the next three songs for some reason. I think "Getting Better" is a little monotonous. The background vocals are unusual but a tad repetitious, and that lead guitar pounds away until I want to scream. I like the verse section, which is well sustained on one chord by Paul's excellent bass and Ringo's flowing rhythms. McCartney, who does not come off well in spontaneous interviews, is quite articulate when forced to organize his thoughts in a song. His "Getting Better" lets him play around with a line, stretching and drawing it out until he's said what he has to say. All in all, that high falsetto, coupled with an overstressed rhythm, wears down my patience.

"Fixing a Hole" is a little less manic. It has the expected drug connotations, brought on by the references to letting one's mind wander. The central metaphor is one of a closed space, of isolation. Perhaps McCartney is commenting on the new role the Beatles have assumed, that of studio musicians, of men now committed to finding themselves and their own sense of meaning in life. Whatever the interpretation, the song churns right along, supported by Ringo's creative drumming and a marvelously rich lead guitar solo.

A footnote to the *Sgt. Pepper* album came to light after the tragic death of Beatles road manager, Mal Evans, in January 1976. Shortly before his death he recorded an interview in which he stated that he had written parts of "Sgt. Pepper" and "Fixing A Hole." Both John and Paul confirmed his statement. Quiet, smiling Mal had actually written the title tune to the Beatles' most famous album.

I think "She's Leaving Home" should have stayed home. It is awfully slow, and Paul's voice, excellent as it is, seems to have trouble hitting and holding some of the notes. Here again, as in "Eleanor Rigby," he is writing in the third person, although the chorus speaks in the first person. The strings and harp are almost too much but are kept interesting by constant shifts in their accompaniment. During the line "our baby's gone," the violins shift from a smooth melody into an alarming series of staccato chords. At another point, in the line "She is having fun," the strings slide wittily into a major seventh chord, the musical equivalent of cocking one eyebrow. The falsetto of the chorus is quite well handled, due mainly to John's wonderful interpretations of the laments of the saddened parents. I suspect that there's a great deal of comedy in the irony of the lyrics. Lennon's wry "bye, bye" refrain, and the "We never thought of ourselves"/"How could she do this to me" contrast deflate the song of some of its pomposity. One flaw, apart from its oversentimental arrangement, is the rather abrupt transition from the end of the chorus back to the final verse; this is really more of an arrangement and recording error than a songwriting one. I think that, in the context of the era, "She's Leaving Home" can be heard as a sly comment on the hippie movement and its effect on middle-class morality.

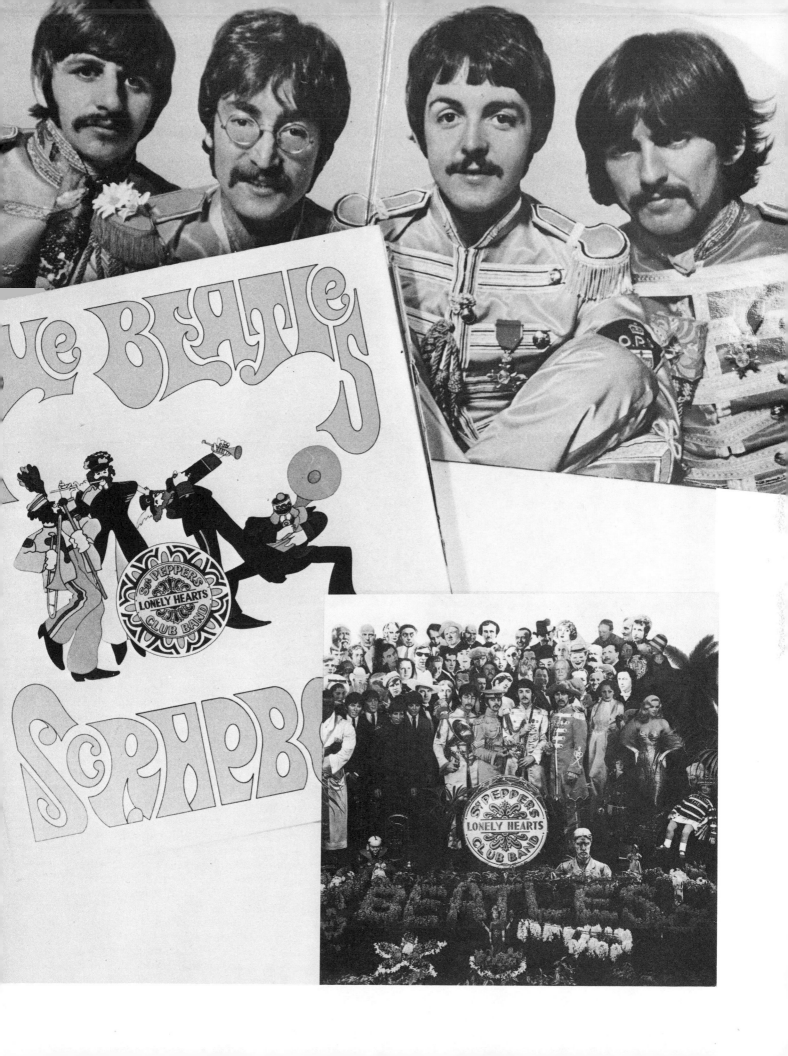

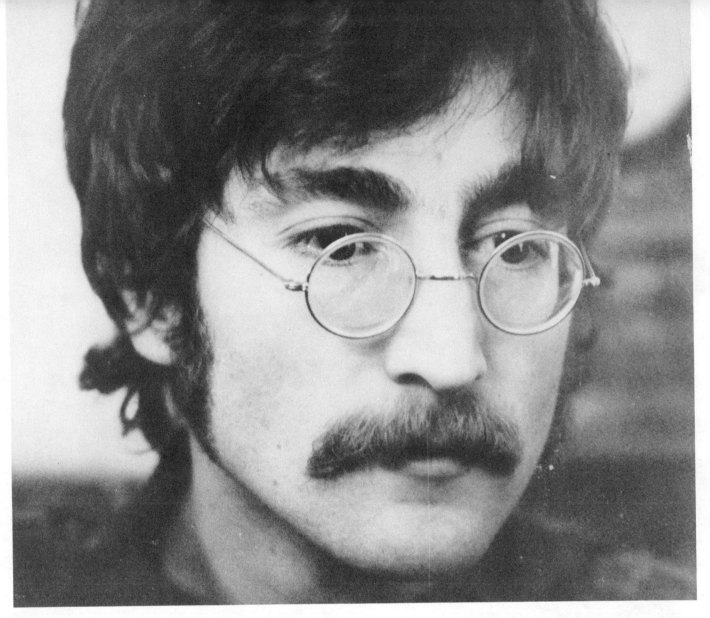

John met Yoko Ono in London, where the Japanese artist staged events such as one in which the audience snipped away pieces of her clothing (opposite top); also a filmmaker, her "Bottoms" featured 365 famous derrières (opposite bottom).

Good old John interrupts the "amen" feeling with his delightful "Being for the Benefit of Mr. Kite!" It is a surrealistic piece; the real is wrenched from its normal place and put into an unusual setting under bright penetrating light. Lennon admits that his source for the lyrics was an old circus poster, but great art is sometimes merely selectivity, and John has selected wisely. He has captured in the sound of his song the undercurrent of the sinister always present in a carnival. Apart from the multilevel organ and celeste tracks there is the distant, delicate snowflake sound of a wind chime. The sudden shift to a waltz tempo echoes "Lucy in the Sky," as do Ringo's carousel cymbals. We can hear the ghostly wailings of a circus organ, almost as if the machine is haunted or mad. Lennon changes keys when it suits him, enhancing the feeling of loss of control. The lyrics don't bother to rhyme, a prosaic shift from John's former devotion to Dylanesque songwriting. The ending is like mayhem in

a music box shop: All the organs take off in their own directions, generating a staticky otherworldliness, until the song ends abruptly in jangling, offbeat confusion.

Most of the criticism of *Sgt. Pepper* places "Within You Without You" at the low spot in the charts. I disagree; I think it is much more interesting than, say, "Getting Better." It fuses elements of Hindu philosophy with a quotation from the Bible—step right up, folks, East meets West right here on this album. The drone of this long song (at five minutes and three seconds, the same length as "A Day in the Life") is hypnotizing, working its spell through the endless variety of improvisation found in Indian music. The middle section is a tasty raga in 5/4 time, a difficult rhythm to sustain, although Eastern compositions sometimes carry as many as seventeen beats per measure! I don't believe George fit the lyrics as carefully to the music as he might have, although "if they only knew" reaches an agonizingly high note. The pun on "without," meaning "outside" as well as "lacking," is worthy of Lennon. It's interesting that "When you've seen beyond yourself" is the very meaning of transcendental meditation, which shows the influence Indian philosophy had on George even before he met the Mahari-

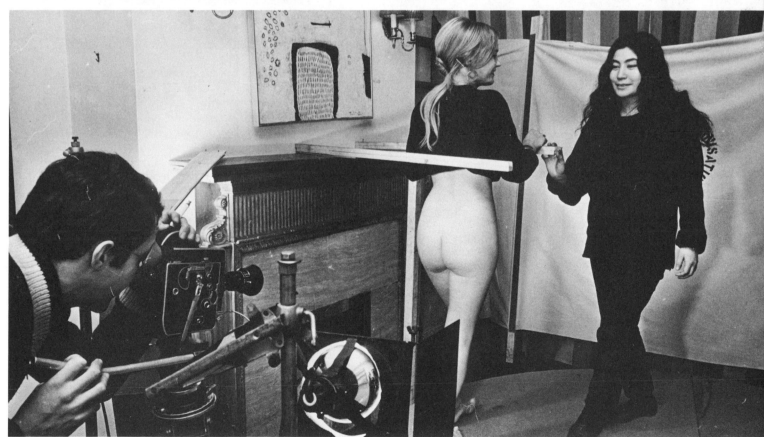

shi. The bizarre laughter at the end scrubs away any excess solemnity that has accrued, but it also is a biting comment on those who listen to the truth but do not hear.

"When I'm Sixty-four" aches to be a classic, and it is. It was written, surprisingly, in Liverpool in the early Sixties, when the Beatles were playing in the now-famous Cavern, and was doctored up and trotted out for *Sgt. Pepper*. It reflects the music-hall influence Paul felt from his father. The subject matter is surprisingly bourgeois for such an avant-garde album, an observation that applies to "Good Morning, Good Morning." George Martin, himself a former oboe player, devised a mellow clarinet background for the song, and Ringo contributes a delightful beat, which at one point seems to be a tap dance on the cymbals. Paul's bass is simple and percussive. This was the first song I learned to play by ear on the piano, and I nearly drove everyone crazy playing it again and again, trying to pick out the melodies.

There is no gap of time between "When I'm Sixty-four" and "Lovely Rita"; indeed, there is hardly a second of silence on the whole record. (Even the very inside groove on Side Two of the English version of this album has a garbled but discernible surprise recorded on it.) "Rita" tumbles in on the strength of Paul's

vocal, propelled by Ringo's persuasive, deep-throated drumming. It's a cleverly written song and one of the best-played instrumentally on the album. There's even an exhilaratingly jazzy piano solo that I would bet was contributed by the flashing fingers of George Martin, who also arranged those jack-in-the-box violins that pop in every now and then. If you listen carefully (it takes earphones), you can hear the chorus sing first "Lovely Rita," then later, "Love *me* Rita." The "chuck-a-chuck-a" backup turns into a lecherous panting during the long coda, then into erotic grunts and groans which end with a long climaxing sigh and an abrupt "Leave it!"

"Good Morning, Good Morning" is a neglected song. The music and instrumentation are gloriously complex, the lyrics likewise. It features one of the best uses of gutsy saxophones on a Beatles record, second only to "Savoy Truffle." Lennon has taken an ordinary subject —the wife, the kids, the day at work—and infused it with an energetic, hectic current of life. Only a brave man would rhyme "clock" with "dark," and "doing" with "ruin," but John pulls it off successfully. A seemingly mundane existence of teatime and clock watching has a substratum that promises more excitement—after a while you take a walk. Forgetting the wife and kids, you flirt with a pretty girl passing by—"now you're in

East meets West: Ravi Shankar (left) taught George
sitar and popularized Indian music, as far as possible,
among rock fans. (Opposite) The Shankar clan prior
to George's 1974 U.S. tour.

gear." When you go to a show, you hope she goes. Lennon even includes a subtle pun, "Somebody needs to know *the time*, glad *that I'm* here." The music shifts from phrases of 3/4 time to 5/4 to 2/4, or if you add it all up, one phrase of 10/4. The chorus is a standard 4/4, however, punctuated by a shotgun drum riff. A cacophony of sound ends the piece: The sound of a cat's meow metamorphoses into a dog's bark; a horse's whinny becomes a pig's grunt, and a lion's roar is transformed into an elephant's trumpet. I always get a Dickensian image when I hear that carriage and its hounds emerge and fade, its trumpets blaring happily.

A chicken's cluck segues into a whiny guitar. There is a faint voice saying "Bye!"; then Ringo gives us a glorious eight-bar downbeat, and off we go into the reprise of "Sgt. Pepper." The lyrics are full of every stage cliché: "We hope you have enjoyed the show"; "We'd like to thank you once again," but the repetition of the line "Sergeant Pepper's lonely" begins to sound as though it were written "Sergeant Pepper *is* lonely." The song makes a necessary key change, then after McCartney lets fly with a ringmaster's babbling cry and a weary "wooh!" slows down for the encore.

"A Day in the Life" is the triumph of the Beatles' career to that point. In 1971 it was voted the best rock song of the past twenty years by three hundred Los An-

geles radio people. It is also listed as the best pop song in a book called *The Best and the Worst* (*Sgt. Pepper* earns a nod as "best pop album"). The apocalyptic vision, the beautiful bleakness of the piece, seem to me on an aural par with Eliot's *The Waste Land*.

The arrangement is sparse and terse: An acoustic guitar (not electric, as on the rest of the album) and piano frame a bare, echoing vocal, as if the singer were standing alone in a vast empty hall. Even the percussion is, at first, spineless; simple maracas shake out a beat. But soon drumming that can only be called majestic ties the lines of the verse together. The lyric is almost agonizingly simple—no imagery, no frills. In a masterstroke of purity, Lennon refers to a film about winning the war (*How I Won the War*?): "a crowd of people turned away." The perfect horror of the film is clear; we don't need to see any of it to understand. The two-note whine of "turn you on" cues the chaotic, chromatic orchestral ascent. Instruments race and tumble over each other to reach that highest chord, while a steady beat (listen for it) continues quietly underneath.

The second section features a stylish softened vocal by Paul, as if he were singing through a thick cloth. There is a boogie-woogie city rhythm to the piece, creating a feeling of frantic urgency. You can even hear someone pant-pant-panting as he realizes he's late. On board the bus he has a smoke, an innocuous reference which the BBC decided had drug overtones. It subsequently banned the song.

Lennon soars in again for the third part of the song. I always think of clouds and flying when I hear the solid chords and full-bodied *aahs*. His voice drifts airily from speaker to speaker, creating a real sense of motion. Loud horns take us down to the final part of the song, similar to the first but more upbeat. After a brief vision of holes in Blackburn (drawn from no more unusual a source than the *Daily Mail*, which ran a story about a Lancashire councillor who, deploring the state of the roads in his county, personally counted the holes in each one), back we go to the hivelike crescendo and that final chord of solid despair. It takes forty-five seconds for it to vanish, during which a squeaky chair can be heard, only slightly reducing the perfection of the recording. (McCartney says that there is also an ultrasonic tone at the very end, as a message to his sheep dog, Martha. A friend of mine *swears* he can discern Harrison saying, at one point in the album, "I'm so bloody stoned. . . .")

Sgt. Pepper changed my life. I saw there was more to pop music than adolescent love songs set to nasal guitars and a beat. There was beauty, poetry and the potential for complex arrangement. As if driving a wedge through a rock wall, the album even got a three-sentence review in the *Kansas City Star*—the first "pop" (as opposed to jazz) record it even acknowledged. "Their elders have recognized reluctantly that John Lennon and Paul McCartney of the Beatles can write a lasting tune." Huzzah and laud, acceptance at last.

My family visited San Francisco that summer to attend my grandmother's funeral. The hippie flower movement of the Haight- (later changed to "love") Ashbury district. was in full bloom. I remember riding through the city, staring like a popeyed tourist, trying to catch glimpses of bearded, guitar-playing men and beflowered, deflowered braless women, supposedly living in a sexually promiscuous narcotic haze.

"There's one!" I cried, pointing as happily as if I'd spotted a yellow-bellied nuthatcher. My aunt, who rued the invasion of her city by the hordes of tuned-in, turned-on dropouts, sniffed in angry disdain.

George lent some dignity to the peace children by visiting them in their natural environment. After a brief stop in Los Angeles to introduce Ravi Shankar to the public ("Indian music makes God come through in a spiritual way. It makes one more aware that God can be put into sound," said George), he walked the streets of San Francisco wearing a deep-purple velvet jacket embroidered with silver thread, purple trousers, and obnoxious heart-shaped sunglasses. "There is a good idea there [in San Francisco]," he told reporters, "but there are also some people who aren't doing what they ought to."

The high priest of hippiedom was Timothy Leary, an LSD-soaked former lecturer at Harvard, who sang the praises of the drug. He wrote proclaiming the Beatles as Four Divine Gurus, "the wisest, holiest, most effective avatars that the human race has yet produced." The Beatles and Leary had one point in common: LSD. The Fab Four publicly announced that they and sixty-one other leading Britons had formed a group to study "heightened mental awareness with special reference to the effects of pleasure-giving drugs." In a full-page ad in the London *Times* the group (which included two members of Parliament) voiced its support of the legal-

The Beatles seldom appeared in public after 1967; souvenirs (below) symbolize the changes 3 years can bring. (Opposite) George's wife Patti was the one who introduced him to Indian culture.

ization of marijuana. John, Paul, and George declared that they had experimented with LSD as a "personal experience to find out what it was like." Lennon said, "We were not taking it for kicks but were trying to find out about its potential for ourselves."

In August 1967 the Beatles were still searching for themselves. Their experimentation with drugs turned into a self-confessed blind alley; they then dabbled in meditation, which was more of an answer but still not *the* answer. While they were struggling with chemicals and philosophy, I was spending the rest of the summer mowing the neighbors' lawns at three dollars a shot. I wasn't exactly going to be able to retire at fourteen, but the income from that, plus what I earned from odd jobs for my father, kept me in science fiction and sunflower seeds. I even bought an occasional record—the Mamas and Papas turned me on with "California Dreaming," and I started collecting albums by the Monkees.

The Monkees were a phenomenon unequaled in entertainment history. They were four guys who hadn't known each other before, pulled together through an audition; they couldn't even sing or play instruments. Don't worry about that, boys; NBC will fix you up. Each week they romped through a half-hour TV show filmed in the style of *Help!*, right down to the use of comic-book titles on the screen. I remember kicking myself after the release of *Sgt. Pepper*, because I realized I should have been collecting Beatle records and paraphernalia. When the Monkees came along, I started snarfing up their records and trading cards in the hope that they might one day be as valuable as I knew the Beatles' would be.

The Beatles had their half hour of television a week, too, only it was in the form of a series of animated cartoons. Their "voices" were not at all close to the originals, since the producers feared Americans wouldn't be able to understand Liverpudlian accents. The caricatures were rather poorly drawn, the figures stiff and unnatural. Each cartoon was structured around a Beatle song, and there was a sing-along in the middle of each program. The show had started in 1965 and held on into 1967, but the time for that sort of thing had passed.

Meanwhile life was flowing on within me and without me. Within me was an increasing sense of maturity and growth. Heck, I'd even passed notes back and forth with *two* girls in my math class. I kept the notes for years afterward: tightly wadded, intricately folded things about the size of a small saltine, filled with strange and misunderstood expressions of a new and unknown emotion. This wasn't love, really; it was young kids going through the motions of what they thought was love. But I remember that hollow feeling I got whenever one of those notes was squeezed into my hand or dropped onto my desk. How would I answer? What would I say? It never mattered; you could get away with any old nonsense in a note.

I bravely signed up to attend the "computer date" party for ninth-graders at the end of the year. I struggled over the application form, answering as honestly as I could but trying not to make myself sound too much like a double-blank domino. I had all sorts of horrible visions: My date would turn out to be a real

bowwow, and I'd be stuck with her all night without a leash, or else I'd get the school's head cheerleader who would take one look at my ears, burst out laughing, and abandon me to seek her own level. I arrived at the party all spiffed out in my suit coat with an emblem embroidered in gold thread on the pocket and my stiff white shirt and my fake necktie. They handed me my card at the door—shock! surprise! wonderment! The computer had given me Match-up Number *One!* Number One! Me? An omen, I thought! An augury of a successful evening! It turned out my partner was neither something more normally found under a rock, nor was she Elke Sommer in a rah-rah suit. She was a nice, average girl, a perfect match for a nice, average guy. We danced a few dances, talked a little, and then made excuses to each other to get away early. The worst part of the whole thing was answering my parents' questions when I got home. "Who was she? Was she pretty? Did you dance?"

And life was flowing on without me. The hippies and their outlandish ways had little chance of penetrating the Republican Midwest. Drugs, to me, were aspirin and

Contac, none of those exotic-sounding happy capsules. The only flowers I wore were in my lapel, where they belonged; the only grass I ever saw was of the type that had to be mowed every other Saturday. There was no danger of my becoming a dropout and flitting away to the magical West Coast, although I confess I felt a secret inner sympathy with the peaceful, free-sounding existence the papers told us was out there.

I was totally confused by all the meditation mish-mash. The Beatles' highly publicized sessions with the guru, who described the Beatles as "very intelligent and young men with a very great potential in life," made me think the group was just trying to see how far they could go. I didn't care. As long as they continued to produce music with the quality of *Sgt. Pepper*, it was all right with me if they wanted to sit on an Alp and contemplate their toes for the rest of their lives.

With the death of Brian Epstein on August 27, 1967, the Beatles faced a crisis from which they never fully recovered. That story and its consequences close one chapter of their lives and open a new and eventually climactic one.

1968

*. . . when the world spun in endless revolution
and the walrus gently wept
and all the sad songs were made better . . .*

The floors of Shawnee Mission North High School are laid with gray linoleum; the walls are half faced with gray fired blocks and half painted in rancid-butter yellow. There is a hallway we used to call "greaser's alley" because it led to the automotive and shop classes. To descend that depth, Dante-like, without a reassuring Virgil at your elbow, was as much of a risk as going on a safari in a sunsuit. There were halls, lined with dented lockers and neutral beige doors, that were confusingly alike and monotonously sterile. Somehow, though, during my three years there, the place seemed to shake with life. So much was going on, there was so much to draw from, that I soon forgot about being a "dumb sophomore" and really started enjoying life at school.

Although it took some time, I finally caught on to the procedures and traditions. I learned where all the rooms were and that no matter what the seniors told you there was no Room 100-X. I figured out that there was no student elevator, either, and any senior who tried to pawn off a ticket on you was just stealing your milk money. I learned not to walk across "The Indian," a floor-tile profile of our school symbol slapped on as an afterthought at the busiest section of the main hallway. If you should happen to brush a corner of the thing with the heel of your Hush Puppies, some overzealous (and oversized) senior was likely to knock you careening into the school trophy case. I tried to do everything right: I bought the activities card, went to all the football games, and joined clubs, clubs, clubs. Pep club (go team!), computer club (soon dropped, however, when my sister said, "That's not cool"), debate club, creative-writing club, and French club.

The last was the most embarrassing, because we all had to sit around and smile politely at each other and speak nothing but *le français*. Conversations were thus minimal, mostly of the "Hi, how-are-you-what's-for-lunch" sort. We did take some field trips, though—we ate at a French restaurant, saw Marcel Marceau in concert, and went to hear Maurice Chevalier in his umpteenth "final" appearance. I remember old Maurice particularly well because during one of his

numbers he embarrassed himself and us by slapping on a dusty old Beatle wig and doing an old man's version of the twist. His well-meaning but geriatric "yeah-yeah-yeahs" managed to burn what few bridges there were over the generation gap.

The experience brought into focus how much ground the Beatles had covered since those "yeah-yeah" days. They were now respected and dynamic innovators who had left the husks of their moptop image far, far behind. As if to prove it, they posed for pictures, their long manes and "hippie" mustaches popping incongruously from the necks of their old collarless gray suits.

Ringo burrowed further into the responsibilities of suburbia when his second son, Jason, was born in August 1967. Maureen's stay in the hospital prevented

The Beatles revolutionized music history with Sgt. Pepper; *then, in 1968, turned to simpler, more basic styles which revealed their individual strengths and weaknesses. (Above) My alma mater.*

(Above) I made a rotten hippie; Nehru suits and peace chains were considered bold for suburban Shawnee Mission, but that's as far out as I went. (Opposite) The Beatles harken to the Maharishi.

him from joining the other Beatles immediately on their excursion to Bangor, Wales, to sit at the foot of Maharishi Mahesh Yogi and catch the cultured pearls of wizened wisdom falling from his whisker-veiled lips. In Wales, however, the circuslike atmosphere of reporters, locals, fans, and the faithful prevented the Beatles from achieving any truly satisfactory results.

The carousel crashed to a halt when a phone call to the Beatles in their meditation camp informed them of the death of Brian Epstein. Brian had been expecting a happy weekend with some new friends, but plans had somehow been snarled. He went home, depressed, and took his normally large dose of sleeping pills. The possibility of suicide was ruled out by doctors, who noted the cumulative effects of the drugs already in Brian's sickness-weakened system. That, probably coupled with the increasing sadness over his lessening importance to the Beatles, resulted in his death on August 27, 1967.

Because the Beatles were surrounded by countless reporters at the meditation scene, their reactions were recorded immediately. "It's a great shock and I'm very upset," Paul said. "We don't know what to say," a subdued John commented. "We loved him and he was one of us."

George took it all very philosophically. "You can't pay tribute in words. Meditation is comfort enough to withstand something like this. There's no real such thing as death anyway. It's death on a physical level, but life goes on everywhere. And you just keep going, really. So the thing is, it's not as disappointing as it seems to be. The comfort is to know he's okay."

The Beatles planned to further their mystic studies by following the Maharishi to India later in September. Plans were again changed when they decided to finish a long-standing project, the film and record of *Magical Mystery Tour*. In Brian's absence, Paul had begun to take over the responsibility of getting the boys together to work. George and John, somewhat less self-disciplined, went along with only moderate enthusiasm. From the tentative beginning *Magical Mystery Tour* was Paul's baby. He plotted the structure of the film, instigated recording sessions, encouraged the others' contributions, and organized the production end of things. His main error lay in what had always been a Beatle misconception: They always wanted instant everything, like instant coffee. They thought it was no trouble to get a forty-two-piece orchestra on a day's notice. Paul thought he could just walk into a studio and bash out a film—a week's project, however, that took six months.

Fate was against any hope for *Magical Mystery Tour*'s success. A movie originally conceived as a theatrical release was shown on tiny British TV screens; a film which, to make its impact felt, depended heavily on a *2001*-like use of color substitution (although *Tour* was made before Kubrick's film was released) was broadcast in boring black and white. Critical reaction is now legendary for its unanimous condemnation. A British friend told me, "We all sat around at Christmas to watch it, thinking, Ooh, Beatles, but it was just dull." Another English friend thought it was "ten years ahead of its time." But the Beatles had failed artistically for the first time in their careers.

The songs, released as a set of two 45-rpm records in England, came out in December as a full-fledged album in America, fleshed out with the other Beatle singles from 1967. I was doing my Christmas shopping in Kansas City's famed Plaza district when the oddly colored sleeve, bursting with clouds and stars, caught my eye from a Woolworth's window. When I'd finally deciphered the hard-to-read Beatles logo, I felt that John, Paul, George, and Ringo, in their animal costumes and chorus-line pose, had gone stark staring bonkers.

I was itching to hear the thing but was on a very limited Christmas budget. So I bought the record as a Christmas gift for my sister, with the condition, however, that she not take it away with her when she went to college the next fall. Some gift. Anyway, I played the album constantly throughout the Christmas vacation.

One night just before New Year's I was sitting in the living room listening to "The Fool on the Hill" and chopping away at a glass of orange juice I'd stuck in the freezer that morning. Snow was falling outside, piling up on the windowsills, nudging its way into the crooks of tree branches. My father came in and gently asked me to go up to his room for a little while. Clutching my little glass, I complied, wondering as I mounted the stairs what was happening. Dad closed the door behind him—something he seldom did when he worked

at his desk. The glow from the lamp made his round face look full and golden-colored.

After a minute or two of chatter I realized where all this was leading. This was that moment every parent anticipates and fears, and that every kid dreads.

The Facts-of-Life Lecture.

Oh, God, I said to myself. This is his big moment as a father. Here he is, doing his duty, bravely following through on his responsibility to me as his son.

And I knew it all already.

I hadn't gone through four years of Boy Scouting and three years of junior-high gym classes with my eyes shut and my ears plugged. I knew at least the rudiments of the procedure, although I'd never had the opportunity of putting them to any practical use. But he was being so great about the whole thing, and I felt so much love for him at that moment, that I couldn't say anything. I sat, my head bowed in a respectful and attentive pose, while the sounds of the *Magical Mystery Tour* album bubbled up through the floor. I stared at my orange juice, hoping to make it last the whole lecture, but it gave out, and I had to focus more attentively on his warm, smiling face and his soft, expressive hands.

I learned more about fathers that night than I learned about birds and bees.

Afterward I went outside to join my friends who were sledding down our street. It was cold and blowing, but my head was still hot from the quiet talk upstairs, and I still tingled where his arms had hugged me. My body was racing down the hill, but my mind was a thousand

miles away. And somewhere in the background, as if providing a sound track to a film about growing up, the Beatles played and sang.

Magical Mystery Tour is an oddly inorganic pastiche of things, an album of fragments. I find it even more "psychedelic" than *Sgt. Pepper* because of the incohesive styles and bizarre twists the pattern of songs takes. The title tune has a great punch to it, with its fanfare trumpets and lyrics lifted, like those of "Mr. Kite," from an advertisement for a real (but unmagical) mys-

tery trip. It features a typical endless ending, with everyone in the studio pounding away on whatever noisemakers they could find. "The Fool on the Hill" is a minor classic. Its trio of recorders and the bass harmonica are nice flourishes, as is the bright, full-sounding guitar.

"Flying" is (ta-da!) the only four-way Beatle composition on record. This is odd, because the piece is so darned simple, an improvisation on three chords. It sounds like something they just hacked out in the studio when they had nothing better to do. If you listen, you can pick out all four voices da-daing away during the third "verse," with Ringo boldly taking the lead. "Blue Jay Way" is an Eastern-flavored song done in a Western style: The humming of a tamboura is replaced by a steady organ overlay. I've always interpreted the "don't be long" line as a punning comment on the "don't drop out" school of thought: "don't belong, don't belong, don't belong. . . ." Also notable are those weird background vocals that drift in and out like the stars you see when you bump your head.

"Your Mother Should Know" is sweet but disposable, as is "Hello, Goodbye," an exercise in dialectic. I could also do without "Baby You're a Rich Man," to my mind the worst Beatle song since they recorded "Mr. Moonlight," way back in 1964. ("Mr. Moonlight," incidentally, was voted worst Beatle recording of all time in a poll of Los Angeles radio listeners.) The best contribution that "Baby You're a Rich Man" makes to Beatle lore, as I see it, is the group's musical announcement of their abjuration of drugs: "What did you see when you were there?/ Nothing that doesn't show." "Tuned to a natural E,/ Happy to be that way./ Now that you've found another key,/ What are you going to play?" The Beatles found, through their own experiences and through the death of Brian Epstein, that drugs were not an answer. Anyone who doubts the sincerity of their commitment need only listen to this song.

"All You Need Is Love," dashed off by John as a simple message for a broadcast of "Our World," begins with "The Marseillaise," followed by a love march. Well, sort of a march, anyway, one that you'd trip over when you came to those measures of 3/4 time stuck here and there in the score. The lyrics suffer from the same haphazardness of "Strawberry Fields" and amount to the same feeling of "whatever you're doing is okay with us." The musical quotations during the long fadeout—one from a Glenn Miller song (over which the Beatles were sued), one from "Greensleeves," a bit from "Yesterday," and a sly and not-very-nostalgic clip from "She Loves You"—are witty and delightful indications of the Beatles' awareness of themselves in a continuum of musical time.

"I Am the Walrus" gave me the biggest kick, mostly because of its obscure, Dylan Thomas-like lyrics. I spent an hour once arguing with friends over the "hidden meanings" of the song and explaining the references to them. I had even looked up all the words ("crabalocker" and "snied" don't exist; "semolina" is a coarse flour and "pilchard" is a fish). Of course I had all the answers. I knew the song had to be about capitalism ("Corporation teashirt"), repression ("Mr. city policeman sitting pretty little policeman in a row"),

The Magical Mystery Tour *project was a disastrous excursion into unfamiliar territory: the music was fine, but the film itself, critics said, was silly, frivolous, without energy or inspiration.*

sex ("pornographic/ priestess boy you been a naughty girl,/ you let your knickers down"), censorship ("man you should have seen them/ kicking Edgar Allan Poe"), unsatisfied pleasure seekers ("you been a naughty boy/ you let your face grow long"), and blowhard intellectual pleasure stealers ("Expert texpert choking smokers"). "Walrus" is all of these things and it is none of them. For Lennon it is a string of neat-sounding words sung to a fluid musical interpretation of a police siren. It is nonsense in the purest (non)sense. The walrus may have derived from the blubbery capitalist in *Through the Looking Glass*, but it doesn't matter. It also doesn't matter that parts of *King Lear* (act IV, scene vi) emerge like a radio broadcast on an interfering channel. If you listen carefully, you can hear the following lines recited under the music:

Oswald:	Slave, thou hast slain me. Villain, take my purse.
	If ever thou wilt thrive, bury my body;
	And give the letters which thou find'st about me
	To Edmund Earl of Gloucester; seek him out
	Upon the English party: O! untimely death.
	Death!
Edgar:	I know thee well: a serviceable villain;
	As duteous to the vices of thy mistress
	As badness would desire.
Gloucester:	What! is he dead?
Edgar:	Sit you down, father; rest you.

The fade out of "I Am the Walrus," which sounds like "drop out drop out everybody drop out," is actually "got one got one everybody's got one." Lennon insists on the second phrase: "I ought to know," he says, "I bloody wrote it."

Magical Mystery Tour was presented by Apple, which to me was an odd, meaningless word to appear on a

Beatles' record. But earlier a tiny credit on the very back of *Sgt. Pepper* read: "Cover by MC Productions and The Apple." I was quite curious about what was going on, but soon it was announced that four musicians/artists/fashion illustrators known collectively as The Fool would design clothes for a boutique in London's Baker Street to be named Apple, financed by the Beatles. Although the shop was soon to close after a giant free-for-all giveway, it was a portent of things to come.

John's first solo film effort, *How I Won the War*, in which he switched from Beatling to battling, opened late in 1967 to good reviews. I dragged my brother Robert to see it, although much of the humor and satire went right over our young heads. I remember that Lennon as the myopic Private Gripweed did a particularly good job—I was moved by one scene where he confesses over and over to having dumped out the troop's water barrel while his sergeant, not paying any attention, insists on knowing who was responsible. "It was me! It was me!" cries Gripweed. I keep wishing the film would be re-released, but so far I haven't seen any indication that it might be.

Back at school I was doing well in classes, except for

French in which I kept drawing Cs. One class in which I really shone was biology, where it was possible (and in my case a reality) to earn A-plusses. Far more interesting than dissecting sheep eyes and writing research papers, though, was a pale, frail-looking girl named Sue Lyons at whose lab table I managed to sit every day. When I first noticed her, I couldn't decide if I thought she was pretty or not. About a week later I decided yes, she was the most beautiful girl I'd ever seen. Her hair was blonde, always carefully brushed away from her bright, intelligent eyes. Her smile, which lit up her delicate face like a candle, never faded, and her voice was always soft, so soft it was sometimes hard to hear. Soon I was actually looking forward to seventh period when I would see her in class. The teacher offered extra credit points to anyone staying late to help, and I often volunteered because I knew Sue would be there.

High school has so many things to offer. I was on the debate squad for a while, and got my picture in the yearbook for helping to win a trophy for the team. I earned the school letter by participating in five debate tournaments, although the sweater I had to wear was black to contrast with the white ones worn by the football and basketball jocks. I couldn't even sit on the lettermen's side of the gym during pep-club assemblies. Debaters were the real black sheep of the school.

I was the only sophomore in the creative writing club, to which I submitted my poems and stories for analysis. We published a magazine called *Mektoub*, filled with typically depressing teenage laments and fumbling verse. Four of my efforts were included that year; three of them were Ray Bradbury-inspired exercises in imagery and vision.

I also got a kick out of writing satire, which I'd done since seventh grade. One day a sister high school presented its talent assembly for us. Part of the act was a group which sang some not-very-funny parodies of Beatle songs, one of which was "Football in Green Bay, Wisconsin," to the tune of "Lucy in the Sky with Diamonds." I sat, a little insulted, thinking I could do better than that. I went home and knocked out three parodies of my own. One of them, since lost, was sung to the tune of "Yesterday" and dealt with the sufferings of any "out of it" kid who had failed to watch the previous night's television programs ("TV shows . . . 'Batman,' 'Lost in Space,' 'Hogan's Heroes': if you miss one that's the way it goes; our TV's in the shop, oh, no . . ."). The other two have been preserved in their entirety, and are reprinted here for the consideration of all:

(To the tune of "I'm Happy Just to Dance with You")

Before this show is through you'll see one hundred and two
Of our advertisements on TV

When you're out of gas and running late
Try our super Shell with Platformate
Put a tiger in your tank and you'll go farther
STP will make your motor purr

For a dirty house use Mr. Clean

For bad breath use super action Gleam
For BO Ban takes the worry out of closeness
Head and Shoulder's if your head's a mess

Television ads, oh oh
The longest word—we should hear it more
Is the word that comes from our sponsor
We love advertisements on TV

Avis Rent-A-Car's still second in place
Use Noxema for a creamy face
Alka-Seltzer takes care of whatever ails you,
For less tar and nicotine smoke True

The White Knight will come and clean your clothes
Milk of Magnesia will end your woes
We are such a wealthy advertising comp'ny
We all run home to watch pay TV

Oh oh, there's no ads at all on pay TV
Oh oh, oh oh, oh!

Or if that's not your cup of tea, try this one, to the
tune of "I Saw Her Standing There":

Well you should have seen, her face looked a scream
And the way she danced—no equal anywhere
Her mod mini-skirt didn't fit her—oh,
To dance with her no one dared.

Well she was my date; to the dance we were hours
  late
Her knee-high boots made everybody stare
How could she have known it was formal—ooh,
In a paper dress with a tear?

Well my heart did race
When I saw her face
And those earrings two foot square

Woh well we danced until eight
To get home I couldn't wait
To ditch her before the evening got too late
You know when to stop with the dating—ooh,
When she's mod at fifty-eight!

Okay, okay, so it isn't Jonathan Swift.

The Beatles were keeping up with their own
songwriting as well. "Lady Madonna" came out in
March 1968. I was driving my sister batty then with
my fanaticism over the group. I asked that she notify
me every time the song came on the radio. One morning
we were dressing for school. She came flying into my
room shouting, " 'Lady Madonna' is on!" My unbut-
toned shirtail flapping, I rushed into her bedroom,
nearly tripping over my untied shoelaces. I stood, completely enraptured by the song. I wouldn't let Susie even
stir until it had ended and I'd had my fix for the day,
thank you very much. "Lady Madonna" is an all-right
song, one that never stops moving forward. The piano
and bass seem to be playing a duet, one line ascending
the scale while the other descends. McCartney gives a
soulful edge to his voice, a throatiness that plays well
off the mocking high backup vocals.

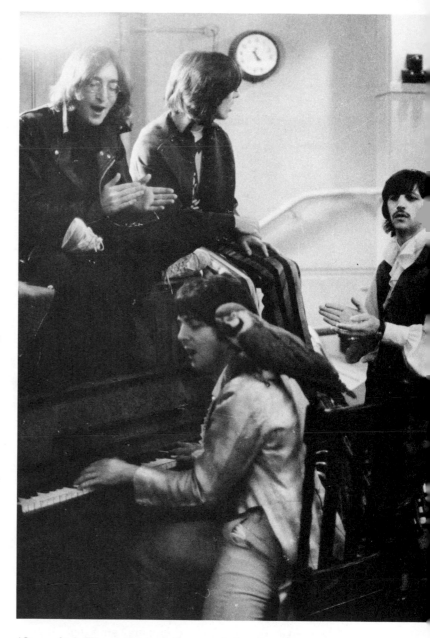

*(Opposite) The mythical image of the Beatles seemed
to grow as the real Beatles (above) withdrew further
into the studio and into themselves.*

"The Inner Light," the flip side, shines like a bauble
on a rajah's finger. It's like a Maharishi lecture set to
music. I think parts of it are quite beautiful—George's
tender vocal, the high flute—and that the song, which
has never appeared on an album, is underrated. It anticipates George's upcoming solo release, "Wonderwall." Incidentally, this single was the last to be released on the Capitol label, and the last to include a
Beatles Fan Club advertising insert.

Summer was a lot of fun that year. It began for me
with the release of Stanley Kubrick's *2001: A Space
Odyssey.* Its coauthor, Arthur C. Clarke, spoke at
Shawnee Mission North, where I met him and asked
him to sign copies of his books. I saw *2001* three times
that year and have seen it many more times since. I
think it's the greatest film ever made, in both style and
content. As I had done with Beatle lyrics, I did with

the movie: hours of thought-stirring discussion and metaphysical analysis. The Beatles were off doing with their guru in India what Kubrick's film was doing for me in a darkened theater: encouraging me to probe my subconscious and develop an outlook on the world and its future.

I was also involved in an unusual summer project. My great-grandfather, John Debo Galloway, was the author of *The First Transcontinental Railroad*, long recognized as a vital reference work on the subject. His research materials had been preserved, and it fell to me to organize and assimilate the hundreds of photographs and documents. I turned the material, plus other books and sources, into a three-part educational filmstrip on the history of railroading in the United States, in time for the centennial of the driving of the Golden Spike.

Once the filmstrip was completed I went with the Scouts to Philmont, a ranch in the mountains of New Mexico. Trudging up those hills in the middle of a rainstorm with a fifty-pound pack on my back is not my idea of a good time, but the fellowship of the troop, including my best buddy James, made it worthwhile. Whistling an occasional Beatle song helped lighten the load, too.

I eventually succumbed to the pressures of the fashion world and bought a Nehru suit with my first royalty check from the filmstrips. The Beatles may have been able to get away with hypnotic colors and velvets, but I was stuck with black double-knit. My family and I took a jaunt to the East Coast where I donned the jacket, my medallion, and my white pants and strolled the streets of New York. The only problem was it was 103 degrees and humid. My white turtleneck turned to muck, and the jacket was shed in the interest of self-preservation. I had brought along some of my short stories and took them personally to the editor of *Fantasy and Science Fiction* magazine. He seemed a little surprised by my audacity (it must have been the Nehru jacket), but he agreed to look over my manuscripts. He returned them a few weeks later with a polite "no thanks" and a few suggestions for improvement.

Schooltime rolled around again, but the Beatles made the thought more bearable by releasing "Hey Jude" at the end of August 1968.

It's hard for me to write about "Hey Jude" because it's my favorite Beatle song of all. It's the strongest medicine I know for curing depression; it is at once comforting, relaxing, stimulating, and transcendentally elevating.

That's a tall order, but "Hey Jude" fills it. The song is so simple, so damned pure and simple—perhaps that's where its strength lies. McCartney, who had tinkered with piano songs before, now cuts loose with a song featuring keyboard as its prime instrument. The lyrics are weak but the intensity of the emotion in the

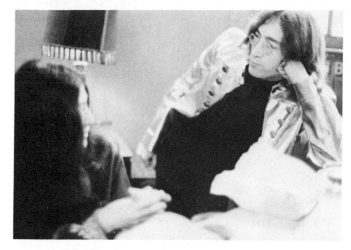

song keeps it vibrant. I believe the song is written as a personal tribute to John from Paul. (The epistle of Jude follows the epistles of John in the New Testament.) The lyrics bear this out. John, exploring his new love for Yoko Ono, is urged to "let her into your heart." Don't be afraid, says Paul, "you were made to go out and get her." Don't save the world, do what you want: "you have found her now go and get her." There are explicit sexual innuendos in the last chorus: "So let it out and let it in," "you're waiting for someone to perform with," which almost seem to foreshadow the *Two Virgins* business.

Whether that's what Paul had in mind or not, I don't know. It doesn't matter. Another interpretation, equally valid and one that makes the song more universal and thus greater, is the simplest one: Be yourself. Be free. There's just you; the world can wait. It's McCartney's salute to everyone on the planet, and he gives it truly cosmic dimensions in the last part of the song. The "better better better" ascent takes off like a rocket, soaring to the highest note Paul can hit; then the song explodes into the "na na na" refrain. It's as if words were no longer needed; there is universal communication in the *feeling*, the *rhythm*, the *sound* of human voices.

I've used the word cosmic; another one that comes to mind is epic. "Hey Jude" seems to span all time, to last forever. The record never really ends; the chorus is singing forever and we just pass by them and catch their song for a few minutes on our separate roads. This all sounds a little heavy, but there's no other way to convey the pure joy the song gives me. I've never been able to listen to it sitting down—it's like a tonic; it moves me physically and spiritually like no other music I know. "Hey Jude" is a magnificent, glorious achievement.

The film of "Hey Jude" made for the "David Frost Show," was shown in America on the "Smothers Brothers Comedy Hour." I talked to a girl who happened to be in London at the time of the filming and who was standing in line to see the premiere of *Yellow Submarine.* She said a man came up to the crowd and asked a hundred people if they'd like to be in a movie; no mention was made of who or what was involved. The lucky hundred were picked up in front of the theater the next day and driven to the studio. Of course they were all pleasantly shocked when they found out what it was all about. They had to do take after take; at the end of each one they all had to go outside again and wait for their cues. It was a long evening, but according to the girl, it was "well worth it." She even got to sit on Ringo's lap for a while. Must have made it awkward for him to play.

"Revolution," the flip side of "Hey Jude," was filmed and shown a week later. It's a great piece of footage, a live recording of a good song. John really lets loose with his overamplified guitar and with a vocal that sounds as if he's shouting in your ear. In the film the Beatles add a few "baum shooby doo wops," and John changes the words a little from the recorded ver-

sion. Overall it has more spirit, really, than the rather clean-sounding single.

"Hey Jude"/"Revolution" was the first release on the Apple label, and it was an auspicious start. The Beatles had expanded the concept of Apple from the original boutique disaster into seven companies: Beatles, electronics, films, merchandising, publishing, records, and television. Apple was to be a gift to the world, an artistic mecca where any good idea would get a hearing. The Beatles sincerely wanted to provide good things for the world at low cost.

They began signing new talent for the record label. They discovered Mary Hopkin, whose high, sweet Welsh voice graced a beautifully Slavic rendition of "Those Were the Days," Apple's first non-Beatle hit. James Taylor released his first album on Apple, and it is a joy—his voice is ethereal, weblike, the arrangements like fine lace. George promoted work by a singer with an oddly nasal voice, Jackie Lomax, whose Apple release is a superior collection of his rocking/tender numbers. One of the best on the record is George's own gem, "Sour Milk Sea." Billy Preston, Doris Troy, The Black Dyke Mills Band—all jumped aboard, the last with a catchy little TV theme, by mentors Lennon and McCartney, called "Thingumybob." There were some accidents, too—Delaney and Bonnie recorded an entire album for Apple. Three hundred copies were pressed and sleeves printed, but it was never released because of contract conflicts. And there was one song by a Scottish group that was censored before it was even released. Despite one or two setbacks, it appeared that the label would be a great success.

Paul and his cohorts were now trying to run financial matters by themselves (and with the counsel of a few friends, including Brian Epstein's brother Clive). They soon found that too many people had their fingers in the Apple pie, that money was being spent on projects doomed to die dismal deaths.

But that wouldn't be for some time yet. While things were good, they were very very good.

I kept up with Apple's progress, but I had other things on my mind as well. I had volunteered to handle the arrangements for the next Boy Scout open house and had been researching the history of vaudeville to find material for a variety show. For three months at the end of 1968 I compiled scripts, rehearsed casts, and accrued props. I even asked James to build a strobe light so we could present a flicker movie live onstage. For titles we used slides taken of cutout letters pasted on a black background, flashing them on the wall at the appropriate moments. In all there were thirteen acts, songs, and skits. After the grand finale the scoutmaster, bless him, mounted the dais and said, "Well, thank God that's over."

That was my baptism by fire in the theater. Earlier, in the spring, I tried out for the high school's production of *The Robe*. It was a spur-of-the-moment thing; I was unprepared and no one in the drama department knew me, but I boldly raced through my audition as if I had a train to catch. I wasn't cast, but that fall I tried again and landed the role of a "townsperson" in *All the Way Home*. Well, it was a start anyway.

Sue Lyons was also in the cast, and by now she had come to mean something very special to me. I was in love; for the first time, I was in love. Every time I saw Sue I went all hollow inside. I thought the temperature in the room dropped by thirty degrees and that the walls started arching in toward me. I loved her face, her hair, her eyes, her delicate mother-of-pearl hands. Poems were all I had to tell her how I felt, but they seemed silly and moon-mad compared to what I really wanted to say.

One night during a dress rehearsal I was sitting in the auditorium in my knickers-and-suspenders costume, watching a run-through of the third act. Sue came and sat next to me, all fitted out in her little-girl's dress. As we watched the show, her hand brushed against my knee and then, like a feather on a stone, stayed there. My head buzzed with hot colors; my eyes darted in and out of focus. My mouth and my brain dried up simultaneously, like ice in a skillet, and I *could not talk*. To make it worse and to make it better, she lifted her hand and gently touched my cheek once or twice. Oh, God, I cried to myself, I haven't shaved and I have this damn makeup on! But she didn't seem to mind. We sat for only a few minutes, but I thought the millenium had come. I somehow managed to make my final entrance, but I might just as well have been gunrunning in the Gobi Desert for all the attention I paid to the play that night.

We rode home in the same car, I in the back seat, she in the front. I couldn't say a word the whole time. As we turned up my street I tentatively touched her shoulder, as though she'd break if she felt too much weight. I know I must have walked through the front door of the house, but I don't remember touching the floor. I was sure sparks were arcing off the tips of my ears.

That Saturday, the closing day of the show, I was shopping with my mother for a new coat. By the checkout counter of a music store I saw a sign that said: "Beatles," and I dashed over to investigate. It was their new album, a two-record, twelve-dollar monster in a plain white cover. My mother smiled indulgently and bought it for me, "as an early birthday present." The number stamped on my album was 0664349—I have the only White Album #0664349 in captivity! By the time I got home with it I had to rush off to school to get made up—there was no time to hear any of it at all.

Apple welcomed talent like Mary Hopkin (opposite top and, far left, with John and Yoko at an Apple Christmas bash) but wasted money on fruitless inventions and a pop boutique in Baker Street (left).

And that night was the night of the cast party, so I wouldn't be able to listen to it until the next day. Oh, well, something to look forward to—something besides going to the party where Sue would be.

I must admit I was not at my suave best that night. During the performance I was sweating but not because of stagefright. It was because of fear that Sue wouldn't want me hanging around her all night. At the party I was just too young and green to handle the situation with any degree of aplomb whatsoever. My conversation was like snow, light and inconsequential, drifting here and there, then melting away. I couldn't be witty and amusing, or sophisticated and dashing. Just a bumble bunny, holding her hand in a corner of the room and trying to dredge up the right things to say.

The party broke up around three that morning. I went home but was too stirred up to go right to bed. I calmed myself down by staring for a while at the lyrics poster that came inside the White Album, trying to figure out in advance what the tunes were to all of those new songs.

It's not an original observation to say that *The Beatles* is really not a Beatles album. It's Paul playing with some musicians, then John with some musicians, and so on. I think it's symbolic that there are four sides to the album, because through it we can see the four sides of the Beatles.

Overall it's a tatty, ragged record, one with many loose, jagged edges. The performances are generally rather poor after the slick professionalism of their last five albums. The songs don't really add up to much, although on an individual basis they are loads of fun. It's as if the Beatles' synergism had vanished—the sum was no longer greater than the parts. I see the White Album as the Beatles' eclectic salute to the history of Western music, though I know they didn't set out consciously with that thought in mind. The record touches on everything from strictly classical arrangements ("Piggies") to straight-out, gut-spilling rock 'n' roll ("Helter Skelter"), from folk ("Blackbird") to blues ("Yer Blues," of course), from country ("Don't Pass Me By") and western ("Rocky Raccoon") to avant-garde ("Revolution #9"), and from Tiny Tim's Music Hall ("Honey Pie") to Chuck Berry's Rock Palace ("Back in the USSR").

I think George Harrison was right when he said he thought it was a mistake to do a four-sided record because people wouldn't be able to get as deeply into it. Although I'm for getting anything at all Beatlish on record, I know I don't play *The Beatles* as often as I would like to, simply because of the time it takes to hear the whole thing.

My favorites on the album seem to be mostly Paul-inspired creations. "Back in the USSR" is a swift little rocker, using the "Lady Madonna" style of singing (in fact, "Madonna" would not be out of place on this album). "Ob-la-di, Ob-la-da" is sheer marshmallow delight, sounding to me like an offspring of "Penny Lane." That reggae beat really churns things up—it's a

good dancin' tune. "Martha My Dear," Paul's love song to his sheep dog, always puts me in a grinning mood, and I like "Mother Nature's Son" the best of Paul's acoustic guitar trio. And for the nostalgic among us, there's Paul's follow-up to "When I'm Sixty-four"—"Honey Pie," with its supermarket trumpets and clarinets.

"Helter Skelter," which is the name given in England to those huge slides found in playgrounds and shopping center parking lots, is dynamite, its resonant fullness of sound giving it an almost noble quality. It's a nice touch when the guitar picks out an eight-note descending scale, as if it were riding down just such a slide. Ringo bashes the heck out of his drums; in fact they all play at maximum intensity, so the cry of "I've got blisters on my fingers" at the end is believable as well as painful.

John's contributions are a little more eccentric. He does well with "Dear Prudence," supposedly written for Mia Farrow's sister who refused to come out to join the meditation sessions in India. "Glass Onion" carries further the idea of looking back on the Beatles' own past; "Strawberry Fields Forever," "I Am the Walrus," "Fixing a Hole," "The Fool on the Hill," and "Lady Madonna" all get a nod. John says he wrote it as a loving acknowledgment of Paul's help in keeping them working together after Brian's passing. "Happiness Is a Warm Gun" is not necessarily a phallic reference, according to John, who found his inspiration for the title in an American gun manufacturer's catalog. It's an-

(Right and opposite) Paul and Ringo clown for the camera; such antics seem out of place when compared to earlier days of Beatle innocence.

other of Lennon's compositions-by-bits, this time somehow turning four songs into one. "Julia" is my favorite of his on the record because of its gentle poetry (it is one of the few Beatle lyrics that reads well as a poem) and wavelike arrangement. It is a loving tribute to John's mother, and the love is very real and very genuine. I hate "Everybody's Got Something to Hide Except Me and My Monkey," with its fire-alarm bell ringing the wax out of your ears. "Hey Bulldog," from the *Yellow Submarine* album, works better in the same idiom. "Cry Baby Cry" has a lovely storybook quality to it. It seems a little unlike John to work in the third person, but he pulls it off.

And then there's "Revolution #9," that Daliesque montage of tape loops and ear-shattering sound tricks. Although no lyrics are listed for the song, there be words aplenty. The very opening has someone calling George Martin a bitch, then *that voice* enters with its jog-trot litany of "Number nine . . . number nine . . ."

Of course there are obvious discernible phrases, but even more fun to find are the ones you have to dig out with earphones and patience. I sat for an hour once, trying to discover something meaningful within all of those bits of reversed tapes, feedback, static, and chanting crowds. The spoken phrases (some by Yoko Ono herself) are so bizarre and non sequitur that I'm still not sure if I heard them right.

Someone who sounds very much like George Harrison talks about a shortage of grain in Lancashire, and a sleepy voice mumbles a morbid monotonic chant, something like: "I couldn't tell what he was saying; his voice was low and his eyes . . . his eyes . . . his eyes were closed . . . his hair was on fire." Then Lennon seems to reply by saying that the wife called and they'd better go now to see he's dead. There follows a discussion of a man who went to see the dentist instead, who gave him a pair of teeth, which wasn't any good, and so instead of that he joined the bloody Navy and went to sea.

And maybe I'm crazy, but it sounds to me as though a man recites a poem with a line like "Here I sit in my broken chair, my twins are broken and so is my hair." There are also references to a man not in the mood to wear new clothing, to a deported headmaster who bought a ticket, and to a nightwatchman with the eccentric habit of carrying onion soup on his person.

What does it all mean? It means John is quite a hand at messing around with thirty tape banks at once, that's what.

George bats .1000, giving us one pretty decent song per side. "While My Guitar Gently Weeps" is his best effort to that point, even though Eric Clapton does play that marvelous solo lead. For a while my favorite song in George's body of work was "Savoy Truffle," a wicked little thing warning of the dangers of overindulgence. The saxophone part bites its way into each line; the organ and electric piano are searing, and George's singing and harmonies are flawless. It's a real nightmare of a song, a bad dream with a sound track. "Long Long Long" is a spacey, ethereal popover that I had to

listen to six or eight times before I finally could hear it. "Piggies" won my favor mostly because of the use of harpsichord, one of my favorite instruments.

And Ringo proudly gives us his first solo composition, the percussion-heavy "Don't Pass Me By." Thanks, Ringo.

And of course there are the throwaways: "Wild Honey Pie," "Why Don't We Do It in the Road?" Unnecessary, but what the heck? I'd rather have them than not.

There was a great stink raised around this time over the release of Lennon's *Two Virgins* LP with its oh-so-shocking, everybody's-gawking, nude cover photograph of John and Yoko. Cynthia had divorced John on No-

vember 8, charging him with adultery. John certainly didn't bother to keep it a secret, releasing this *outré* assemblage of twitters and tweets with a few erotic gasps thrown in for bad measure. The problem with the public was that everyone thought *The Beatles* was the nude album, because it was "obvious" that the plain white cover had to be substituted for the controversial one. There was no connection between the two records whatsoever, just bad timing on John's part. *Two Virgins* achieved instant notoriety and was not available in most stores, although a few years later a record store in Los Angeles was selling a stack of them, literally reaching to the ceiling, for two dollars each; modest indeed, compared to the photo on the jacket.

I couldn't find the record anywhere in Kansas City. During a rehearsal one day, waiting for my cue to go on, I was sitting next to Sue Lyons and Mary Lee Wilson. Just to make conversation I turned to them and asked, "Do you know where I can find *Two Virgins*?"

Mary looked stunned for a second, then looked at Sue and again at me. "Sure," she fired back, "right here, kiddo!"

George Harrison released his first solo album in November, right alongside *The Beatles* and John's masterpiece. *Wonderwall* is an unusual mishmash, combining some Eastern (*very* Eastern) and some Western (*very* Western—one piece is even called "Cowboy Museum") tracks. "Wonderwall to Be Here" and "Singing Om" are hauntingly beautiful cuts. Some of the bits, however, sound, according to my sister, suspiciously like cats being tortured with hot iron spikes. I think it's a good album, although I question just how much George really had to do with it. Some of the music, frankly, sounds too complex for him to have written,

very feminine-looking hair dryers. One man had his hair tied up in little ribbons, like one of the Our Gang kids—apparently he was going to wash that gray away. I almost burst out laughing, but Mario slammed me into an upright position and began whacking away at my shaggy brown locks, insulting my head and my shoes alternately.

Tufts of hair drifted to the ground like miniature fallen timbers. I thought everything was all right until I began feeling a breeze on the northernmost point of my skull. Squinting myopically at Ringo's portrait, I began realizing that *he* probably doesn't feel a breeze.

"You're not taking too much off, are you?" I ventured.

"Relax," the stylist said, as his scissors snipped away.

Eventually he took a hair blower and dried me out. The air it blew was so hot I had tears in my eyes. I started to duck away from its hellish blast, but Mario held me firmly. "Don't move," he said sternly, muttering under his breath.

I'm blind without my glasses, and I couldn't see what he was doing in any of the mirrors around the room. Finally Mario combed me out, dusted me off, and let me see the results.

I was obliterated. Instead of a full Ringoish cut, Mario the Barber (stylist, excuse me) had whittled me down to about the texture of a tennis ball. I looked less like Ringo than did one of his drums.

"Well?" Mario said.

Paul (top left, with Martha) and George experimented with soundtrack composing; John devoted more time to Yoko. (Above) Off to scout camp.

and I think he selected talented musicians to help round out the pieces. If I'm wrong I'd be delighted.

The Beatles were now getting as freakish as they could possibly get. Their Fool-designed clothes went beyond mere psychedelics into the totally outlandish. Their hair was long, longer, longest. I finally decided to do something more radical to my appearance, and so I called for an appointment to have my hair styled. My father had cut it since I was old enough to have hair, but I now wanted to try something new.

I knew I wouldn't be able to describe what I wanted, so I fished around for a picture to show the barber. I noticed Ringo's photo on the inside of *Sgt. Pepper*. Neither of us is particularly good-looking, but I thought his haircut was very flattering. So off I went to the Royal Room Hair Salon, *Sgt. Pepper* under my arm and ten dollars in my pocket.

The barber ("stylist," he corrected me) was named Mario and was not a friendly person. I showed him the picture of Ringo. He looked at me, then at the picture, then at me again. He frowned.

"Problem?" I asked.

"No. But remember, you won't end up looking like that picture. Everybody's head's different."

"I understand," I said. "Is it unusual for somebody to bring in a picture of what he wants?"

"No, no," Mario replied, shoving me into the chair and wrenching a rubber sheet around my neck. "I've just never had a record jacket sprung on me before."

As he shampooed and massaged my scalp (it felt like my hair was being anointed with oil and vinegar, then tossed like a salad), I had time to glance around and drink up some of the environment. Dignified business-men were trying to look nonchalant as they sat under

"It's—uh—great," I said, but not too loudly. I swallowed a lump the size of an avocado seed. "I really like it." What was I going to say, put it back on?

I paid off Mario and left angrily. It'll grow back, I consoled myself. That is, if he hasn't singed it to the roots and stunted its growth. At home I tried wearing dark turtleneck sweaters, my father's old army wire-rimmed glasses—*anything* to camouflage Mount Baldy. Nothing, except a few weeks' time, did any good. It was years before I'd trust another barber, and then only if he had a barber-college diploma, a letter of recommendation from a nationally prominent cler-gyman, and a note from his mother.

1969

. . . when shining slumber kissed our eyes
and golden sunlight came and smiled us into waking
and we saw the something that held us all together . . .

The wildest Beatle year of all opened with the American release of the animated film *Yellow Submarine* in the late winter of 1968. It was a Christmas present better than snow or a stocking stuffed with peppermint. However, there was something more important on my mind.

Once North's production of *All the Way Home* closed, I no longer saw Sue as much as I would have liked. Something, I told myself, had to be done about

The Beatles look a little confused in this publicity shot for Yellow Submarine; *John gives the hand signal used by his cartoon counterpart. (Above) I earned the Eagle, the highest Scout award.*

the situation. Like a nervous Eisenhower organizing a small-scale D Day, I forged ahead with arrangements for my first ever, honest-to-God, by-the-rulebook Date.

That phone call to Sue was the highest Everest I have ever had to climb. I went into the bedroom and closed the door. Shaking like a Waring blender that had thrown a bolt, I looked up her number, although I'd committed it to memory weeks before. I must have dialed the number—or six digits of it—ten times without ever completing it. I probably misdialed, I told myself. Or she's not home. She's busy and doesn't want to talk. Or there's a sandstorm in her neighborhood, and they need to keep the lines open for emergency calls. Actually dialing the last digit was like finger-drawing in partly dried concrete. When I heard the phone ringing at the other end, I shivered but held on. Her father answered. During the silence while Sue was called to the phone, I thought of a hundred quick, stupid reasons to hang up, but my last chip of determination held me there.

She must have sensed the tension in my voice, which sounded as though I'd taken a swig from a cup of sawdust, because she was sweetly encouraging over the phone. She agreed amicably to all the plans, then, after a few moments of idle talk, we rang off. My shirt was soaked, my hands moist and numb. The decathlon runners in the Olympics have it dead easy.

I wish I could report that the evening was a triumph, but it wasn't. Since I couldn't drive yet, I had to ask a friend to chauffeur and pick me up at seven, although I was all shaved and showered by five. We got to Sue's a good half hour too soon. "You're early," she said in a not altogether lighthearted voice, as she dashed around putting on her finishing touches. The show was all but sold out, and we had to sit in the balcony—for practical not romantic reasons. I thought the movie was horrible, but Sue was crying by the end. I didn't know what to do or say; in debate I had done fine when it came to extemporaneous speech, but here I was helpless.

Matters weren't expedited much by riding home with my parents. Their presence didn't make it any

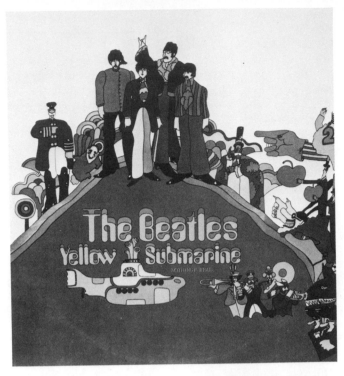

easier to talk to Sue, nor did I want to kiss her good night with them in the car. I had wanted Sue to have such a good time but felt I had failed to make her at all happy or even very comfortable. I went home and brooded about the whole mess until I fell into a desultory sleep.

About the best thing that had happened all night was the theater's showing of a coming-attractions trailer for *Yellow Submarine.* I remember it so clearly: it opened with a deep, ominous voice slowly intoning, "Nothing is real . . ."; then the chimneys of Liverpool, splashed with painted-postcard colors, belched a sooty whistle blast. I leaned forward in my seat, my eyes bulging. "Oh, wow!" I said over and over, while Sue smiled patiently.

The film came to Kansas City in January while Christmas break was still on. My companion and I went to a matinee screening but had gotten our timing confused and arrived in the middle. As we walked into the theater the "Lucy in the Sky with Diamonds" sequence was playing. I was dazzled by the rapid flashes of color and the whirring, mind-spinning changes of image. As we took our seats I whispered to my friend, "I'm going to *like* this!"

Yellow Submarine is not unanimously welcomed into the canon of Beatle celluloid. The project was started to fulfill the Beatles' contractual obligations to United Artists for a third feature film. Originally the Beatles were to play dramatic roles in a Western to be produced by Walter Shenson, but none of the four was interested in putting in the necessary work. An animated film solved the dilemma.

The Beatles myth reaches full flower in the movie. The Beatles themselves were hardly needed at all; they did grind out four new songs for the film, although one ("Hey Bulldog") wound up on the cutting-room floor. And oh, yes, they surfaced briefly for a live and embarrassingly unamusing clip at the end. They didn't even provide the voices for the film, but the voices that were used sound almost more real than the originals. ("We *are* the originals," says the cartoon Paul.)

The film sustains itself in the absence of the Fab Four through daring innovative drawing techniques (Disney was never like *this*!) and a literate script (marred by a badly recorded voice track) by four screenwriters, the best known of whom, Erich Segal, is usually credited with the final rewrite. *Yellow Submarine* is witty, clever, and charming, even if it is sometimes clumsily made and badly edited. A friend of mine thought it was a satire on the Nazis. Ridiculous! I retorted; it's about Blue Meanies.

As my friend and I left the film a blizzard was blustering, turning the streets to frozen lakes and cars to ice skates. That didn't stop me; a sign in the lobby advertised that a local store had the soundtrack album to *Yellow Submarine*, and by God I was going to get it. I was anxious to test my newly licensed driving skills anyway. I made it to the store, slippin' and slidin' the whole way, but the ad was wrong. The album didn't come out until a month later, and I had to wait impatiently.

The four new songs on the sound track seem like leftovers from the hyperelectronic sessions for *Sgt. Pepper*. George contributes the bulk of fresh material.

Yellow Submarine is a dazzling display of animated virtuosity and innovation. The premiere (above and opposite below) stopped traffic in Piccadilly Circus, the third time in the Beatles' career.

"Only a Northern Song," a reference to their music publishers, was tossed off to meet a last-minute recording deadline for the film. Its lyrics, almost lost in a jungle of peanut-butter-thick sound effects, are a nice soft-pedaling of any vestiges of Beatlemania. As if in answer to a boring reporter's queries about his personal life, George sings, "It doesn't really matter what clothes I wear/Or how I fare or if my hair is brown." After all, he seems to say, a Beatles tune isn't divine or oracular, it's only a song. "It's All Too Much" is a long piece verging on the monotonous, but still quite shimmering. It's almost majestic in scope, a feeling well captured by the finale of *Yellow Submarine*. (Interestingly, the film's version of this song contains a verse and a chorus not heard on the record.) I get a kick out of the faint sound of an alarm clock heard just as the song fades away.

George seemed to be the only Beatle interested in *Yellow Submarine*'s success, but Paul did donate a throwaway tune, "All Together Now," featuring John on wheezing harmonica, and Lennon came up with "Hey Bulldog," which did not survive the London premiere. "All Together" is a good kid's song, a risqué nursery counting rhyme set abouncing. "Bulldog" has an excellent piano/bass riff and some oddly non sequitur dialogue toward the end ("What do you mean, man, I already have grandchildren!") John once again shows his powerful agility with words; the lyrics have a sinewy toughness to them.

While *Yellow Submarine* was perpetuating the Beatles myth, the Beatles themselves were starting to see it end. The recording sessions for what eventually became the *Let It Be* album and film began in January, instigated by Paul, who felt the group needed some public exposure. He cautioned that they were becoming too invisible to their fans and suggested they do a major project. "No films," said George, although that is eventually what came out of it. Concerts were out—

too big, not enough people could be served. A TV show? No, said John. Paul suggested they appear at small clubs unnannounced, under an assumed name like "Ricky and the Redstreaks," an interesting idea which never came to anything. They got the public exposure they wanted, to the delight of confused passersby and to the annoyance of nearby bankers, tailors, and civil authorities, when they performed a spontaneous live concert on the rooftop of their Apple offices in Savile Row.

Apple by now was seen by many as a giveaway house. Almost anyone could come away from 3 Savile Row with something, whether cash or a stolen souvenir. George, who was supposed to be the one always so concerned about money, gave away checks to people who needed air fare or food or just an evening out. John and Yoko had appeared as Father and Mother Christmas at a party, but it seemed the party would never end. Money was spent like water, and the company needed help.

Allen Klein, the Rolling Stones' manager, was asked to look into things. Meanwhile, the Beatles abandoned the *Let It Be* tapes and film footage to George Martin and Glyn Johns, another record producer, to pursue their own interests. On March 12 Paul married a New York photographer named Linda Eastman (no relation to the camera family). I don't know if the Kansas City girl who threatened to jump off a building in case Paul

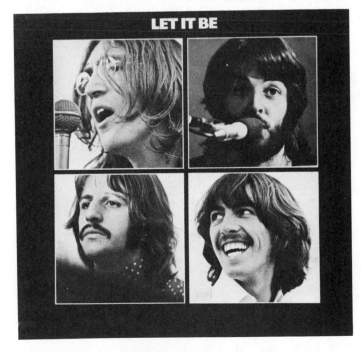

The Beatles rocked London's fashion district with a free midday concert atop the Apple offices in Savile Row. From the session came the hit "Get Back" and the better part of the film Let It Be.

got hitched ever really did jump, but news of McCartney's marital vow was soon swept away in the flood of publicity ballyhoo surrounding John's marriage to Yoko a week later.

Lennon had met the Japanese artist at a museum in 1966. He was intrigued by her unusual conceptual art, which had a kind of childlike beauty to it. For one piece she cut a hole in the ceiling and instructed participants to lie on their backs and watch until a cloud floated overhead; for another she instructed, "Carry a bag of peas. Leave a pea wherever you go." Her work is an art gallery for the mind, which urges the one who experiences it to rediscover the world of the small and the overlooked. Approached with an open mind, her pieces are refreshing, quaint, sometimes even stimulating.

But much of the public refused to be open-minded. They saw only that Yoko was Japanese and that John, however eccentric, was a white Englishman, and traditionalist blood boiled when the two were married. They couldn't believe that John would choose Yoko over any of the more physically beautiful women he might have had. The *Two Virgins* incident and John's subsequent divorce from Cynthia also lowered the couple's public standing.

Their honeymoon was the most publicized and controversial Beatle event since John's religious slip two and a half years earlier. John, always media-conscious,

knew his wedding would be pounced on by the press anyway, so he decided to use the opportunity as an advertisement for peace. He and his wife staged the famous Bed-In at the Amsterdam Hilton, where they literally stayed "undercover" and greeted anyone who wanted to come and talk with them about peace. Reporters seized the hotel, thinking they were to witness a karmic consummation of the marriage but were confused when confronted with a soft-speaking man using his public position to advance a cause in which he believed sincerely.

The Lennons recorded the event on a cassette which eventually became the *Wedding Album*. As if the public had been invited to the ceremony, the album package, not released until November, contained a set of four photo-booth snaps, a postcard, a picture of a piece of the wedding cake in a white plastic bag labeled "Bagism," a poster, a book of surprisingly hostile press notices and cartoons, and an intimate glance at the wedding pictures. The record itself is atrocious self-indulgence: Side One has Yoko saying "John" and John saying "Yoko" 485 times and 485 ways. Interesting for students of oral interpretation but boring for anyone else. Side Two is a little better. There are snippets of interviews, discussions, and music recorded in bed and on the streets of Amsterdam. The idea of an aural documentary is novel, but the subject is tedious. Our stereo was broken at the time I bought the record, so I

(Above) Illustrated books elevated Beatle lyrics to the realm of visual poetry. (Opposite) Portraits from the last Beatles photography session.

took it to a friend's to play. He listened for a while in consternation, then turned to me and said, "If they released an album of John belching for forty minutes, you'd probably rush right out and buy it."

I paused. "Yes," I replied, "I probably would."

Being an all-out Beatle freak, I could forgive John his eccentricities. What I could not forgive was the angry, uncomprehending hatred the public, including some of my friends, felt toward Yoko and John. Sure, maybe he didn't have to be so aboveground, so tiresomely visible all the time, but at least his cause was a good one. And I respected him for finding that love goes beyond beauty and for having the courage to commit himself to his idea of truth. His marriage to Yoko and his subsequent changing of his middle name from Winston to Ono indicated a oneness and a deep, deep feeling too often lacking in relationships, and I was proud of him.

I was not happy, however, with Yoko's music. I like "Give Peace a Chance," a single recorded in bed in Montreal, John's improvisational mantra that hopes to liberate the world from "isms" (bag, drag, rag) and "tions" (revolu, evolu, integra, medita). John even slips "masturbation" in there somewhere but changed it to "mastication" in the printed lyrics. The flip side is Yoko's. She is not gifted with a good singing voice, and her lyrics are ghastly. She does have an adequate sense of melody but a bad sense of song structure. At least this song, "Remember Love," made some attempt to be musical, something you can't say for her later efforts.

I first heard the Beatles' next single, "Get Back," on the radio while pushing the car out of a mud puddle after a dismal camp-out. The song struck me as garbage—"If anyone else had written it, it wouldn't even get recorded," I commented to a soaked fellow Scout—but eventually it grew on me, till now it's one of my favorites. John struggles with a simple but earnest lead guitar solo, and Ringo's one-bar drum solo is one of my pet two seconds of Beatle music. "Don't Let Me Down" on the B side is pretty, especially the middle eight section. It has a fresh, "live" feel to it; in fact the single was advertised as "The Beatles as Nature intended."

"Get Back" came out in April. That month I performed as Reverend Parris in *The Crucible*, my first big role. Our director worked us like Trojans, and the show was very, very moving because of it. Sue was also in the play, but by then I knew there wouldn't be any relationship between us. The realization hurt, and it couldn't help but show. She went to the cast party with her new boyfriend. I had to leave when she arrived. I went home and sat at the piano, playing "And I Love Her" over and over again. Tears fell, as they do now whenever I hear the song.

A friend in the cast was also having romantic troubles. After rehearsal one night, as I drove him home, he

Paul returned to more traditional values by tying the knot with American rock photographer Linda Eastman and adjusting quickly to domesticity.

told me about a girl he loved but who didn't love him. I wished I had an answer to give him, for we were struggling with the same problem. Suddenly some words that the Beatles had sung started echoing in my head:

Your day breaks; your mind aches,
There will be times when all the things she said
Will fill your head; you won't forget her.
And in her eyes you see nothing,
No sign of love behind the tears
Cried for no one;
A love that should have lasted years.

"Go home and listen to the Beatles," I said to him. "They understand, too. They'll share your load."

During rehearsal breaks I had fun getting into bull sessions, which often drifted onto things Beatleish. One fellow in the cast, a particularly brainy guy whose IQ was rumored to be over 180, had very adamant (and usually right) opinions about everything, including the Beatles. "Is George saying, 'All the world is birthday cake' or 'All the world has been vacated'?" we'd wonder. "Is it 'big man' or 'wig wam' in 'Hey Bull-dog'?" One song, "Tomorrow Never Knows," particularly irked him. "You must *never*," he cried, finger waggling in the air, "turn off your mind and float downstream."

Later that month I appeared as a pianist in the school talent show. I was nervous and distinctly un-showmanlike, but I fumbled my way through a medley I'd compiled of "Hey Jude," "Lucy in the Sky," and "MacArthur Park." For a finale I played a new instrumental piece, the first one I'd ever composed, which bore the prodigious (and self-mocking) title "Pseudo-Classical Improvisation #1 in D-minor." It was more Bach- than Beatle-inspired, but it had traces of "Eleanor Rigby" buried in it somewhere.

One Apple record project that got further than most but sputtered to a halt after two releases was the Zapple label. Originally conceived as "paperbacks" of the record industry, Zapple was to have put out mostly spoken-word discs, such as an interview with Pablo Picasso or performances by Lenny Bruce. The cost was to be around two dollars—like a magazine in afford-ability and disposability. But the label, the regular

green label with a silver Zorroish "Zapple" across it, managed to give the world only John and Yoko's *Life with the Lions*, the follow-up to *Two Virgins*, and George's *Electronic Sound*.

Lennon's record is alternately a pain in the heart and a pain in the neck. "Cambridge 1969," constituting all of Side One, is an earsplitting endurance contest between Yoko's yip-yap-yammer and John's screeching feedback guitar. Side Two is a series of cassette recordings from the Lennons' stay in the hospital during Yoko's miscarriage. Yoko sings two newspaper stories a cappella while John chants Gregorianly in the background. In a chilling bit of pained recording we hear five minutes of the baby's heartbeat, then, as abruptly as death, two minutes of silence. George's contribution is a manifestly unmusical collection of whirrs, beeps, and hisses. There is about a minute on Side One where the sound is so intense and penetrating that it makes me think the stereo is intensely hot and melting. The

The Beatles came to depend on each other less and less for musical self-expression. Their separateness is symbolized (above and opposite) as they posed for photographs in London parks.

idea of having an original cover amateurishly painted by a witty George Harrison is actually a rather cute one. On the cartoon wall are hung George's drawings of what appear to be the "White Album" portraits. Below the record player is the frustrated expletive, "Crapple with it."

My school year ended on a suitably Beatle-touched note. I had been voted editor of the literary magazine, and one of my poems that got published had four very deliberate references to Lennon-McCartney songs. And for our final project in English class, after a disastrous attempt to create a film, three friends and I designed what we called a "total environment," in which we assaulted our classmates' senses with movies, textures, scents, flavors, and sounds. I provided the sounds: a tape of the Beatles' most electronic, far-out pieces, including "It's All Too Much" and "Revolution # 9."

The Beatles were awarded another Ivor Novello award for highest sales in Britain, this time for "Hey Jude." I was really irked when "Hey Jude," nominated for a Grammy for best song of 1968, lost out to Simon and Garfunkel's "Mrs. Robinson." There was no excuse for that, I raged; their song is nothing without the movie to give it meaning! "Hey Jude" is for all time,

"Mrs. Robinson" ends when *The Graduate* is over. Grr, grr, grr. At least Simon and Garfunkel acknowledged their debt to the Beatles with a quotation from "I Am the Walrus": "Goo goo g' joob, Mrs. Robinson."

A single called "The Ballad of John and Yoko" came out June 16, but it wasn't really a Beatles single. It was a quickie by John, which had him playing lead and rhythm guitar and Paul on bass *and* drums. The line, "Christ! You know it ain't easy," and a reference to John's supposedly upcoming crucifixion, brought back memories of the Bible Belt Backlash of 1966, and the song was censored on many radio stations. Our local "progressive" FM rock station played the song right at midnight when it switched to a simulcast with AM, so that the banned version would be heard at least once on the airwave of the multitudes. Later the AM stations played a doctored tape of the song, in which the offending word "Christ" was snipped out and reinserted in *reverse*. This kept the beat of the song going, but it sounded like someone kept bumping into the turntable.

The Beatles, frustrated by the delay in the release of *Let It Be*, returned to the studio to record what was to become *Abbey Road*. Encouraged by my musical

progress since I quit taking piano lessons, my father financed the recording of a vanity album, on which I played six original compositions and eight Beatle ones. It's one of those early "artistic" ventures that everyone must have in some form or another and which everyone would just as soon forget.

Summer arrived, and soon my brother and I took off for Europe on Icelandic Airlines with twenty-five other members of Boy Scout Troop 91. It was a glorious trip, made even happier by the use I made of my free time. In London, standing in front of a TV set in Harrod's (the Macy's of Great Britain), I watched the live coverage of Apollo 11's blast-off on the flight that would land two Americans on the moon. When that was over, I made my first visit to the Apple office in Savile Row. The secretary was not pleased to see more tourists arrive at a place of business, but she was used to it and was very helpful. She answered all my questions and gave me some publicity handouts. No Beatles were there that day, but I did get to peek into John's all-white office on the main floor. I left, feeling as though I'd made a pilgrimage to a shrine.

Each boy stayed for a week with the family of an English Scout living in the Chester area, seven miles across the river from Liverpool in the north of England. My host graciously drove me around to see the Cavern Club, 10 Mathew Street, which looked awfully dirty and small from the outside. A hand-painted sign above the door announced, almost sadly, that "The Beatles Played Here 292 Times!" The door was all boarded up; the "Mersey Sound" no longer found a home in the converted wine cellar.

From there we drove under the oppressively gray Liverpool sky to Penny Lane, where I amused my host by snapping slides from every angle. There was the barbershop, which had plastered its window with Beatle pictures and sheet music. I peeked in the window, where a barber motioned at me to take his picture amid the photographs showing all the possible hair styles—"every head he's had the pleasure to know."

John invited the world to his marriage with Yoko through the Wedding Album, *which included a piece of cake, scrapbook, and posters. Knowing the world would watch, the Lennons turned the event into a heartfelt and well-publicized ad for peace.*

There was the shelter in the middle of the roundabout, and a bank on the corner, and a fire station—just as in the song. There was no nurse selling poppies, but I think I just may have spotted a banker on a corner.

While in Europe I blew most of my money on Beatle records. I collected two rare singles, "Obladi Oblada"/"While My Guitar Gently Weeps," and "Back in the USSR"/"Don't Pass Me By," which were European only, never released even in England. Apple told me where to pick up some of their more obscure releases, like "Thingumybob," and I managed to sneak the infamous *Two Virgins* through customs by stuffing it in the very bottom of my Boy Scout duffel bag.

My senior year began auspiciously. Sue Lyons and I were elected by the journalism class as coeditors of the paper, and I volunteered to be the high-school reporter on WHB, the local teen radio station. The creative writing club once more elected me as its president, and I landed a good supporting role in the fall play, *Look Homeward, Angel.* In my spare time I began compiling what I called the Beatle Bible, a complete Beatles' discography and lyrics book. I had to listen to the songs over and over, so I could write out all the "bop shoo ops" and "yeah yeahs," and all the ad-libbed studio bits.

One day in early October, KUDL, the more progressive AM station, played a song that reminded me vaguely of "Yellow Submarine," called "Octopus's Garden." I realized it was Ringo singing, and I called the station to find out what was happening. I had to wait on the line for thirty minutes, but the disc jockey finally answered and confirmed it. The Beatles were about to release a new album, *Abbey Road.*

I went to the record store daily after school until it fi-

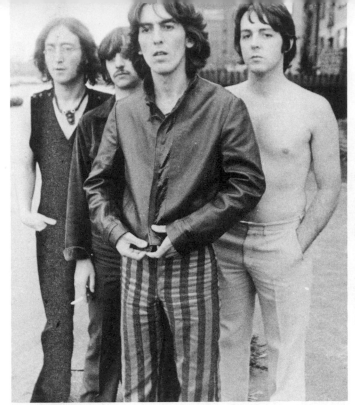

Portraits from the magnificent series by Stephen Goldblatt, the last publicity photograph session the increasingly reclusive Beatles would allow.

nally appeared. It seemed disappointingly simple: no giveaway posters, no lyrics, not even a fold-open jacket. But the music inside was tremendous, and I said so in my review for the Shawnee Mission North newspaper.

Until then *Sgt. Pepper* seemed like the best Beatles album. I listened to one right after the other and concluded that *Abbey Road* has the edge. It is far more truly Beatle-like, the songs are more typical and less dependent on electronic wizardry; the arrangements are all outstanding, their playing is flawless, and their voices are clearer and more expressive than they've ever been.

"Come Together" has sexy nonsensical lyrics that are considerably more serious than the horseplay in "I Am the Walrus." The arrangement is menacing and spidery. "Something" and "Here Comes the Sun" are George Harrison's crowning achievements and the best two songs on the album. Frank Sinatra even paid "Something" the compliment of dropping "My Way" from his permanent repertoire and replacing it with George's song, calling it "the greatest love song of the past fifty years." It is beautifully, achingly tender, especially in the chorus section. The melody is as good as anything Paul ever wrote. As high-school radio reporter it was my job to announce on the air the top three songs at school each week. I always put "Something," the first and only Harrison song released on the A side

of a single, in the number-one spot, regardless of whatever may have been the true favorite. A girl I had a crush on, Suzi Shea, said she always associated this song with me. I was flattered.

"Maxwell's Silver Hammer" is a grotesque little piece, its happy-go-lucky music an ironic counterpoint to its murderous lyrics. It's another McCartney tale in the third person, taken from a true story of a tool-wielding killer. But Paul warns us not to take it seriously by snickering audibly in the second verse. He follows that song up with "Oh! Darling," a throat-ripping rocker that sounds as if it were lifted from Elvis's repertoire. McCartney, a musical perfectionist, rehearsed the song until he made his voice sound as though he had been singing the thing onstage for a week. The rough and pained quality he thus achieved works beautifully.

"Octopus's Garden" is Ringo's second solo composition, with a little help from his friend George. It's cute and harmless and features a bubbly solo by Harrison and a frisky, fishy trio of harmony vocalists. "I Want You (She's So Heavy)" rips into the delicate, gay mood of "Garden" with teeth and fingernails. John's gruff, almost snarling tribute to Yoko, broken into two parts, derives much of its texture from an awesome organ track by Billy Preston. The abrupt cutoff at the end always sounds as though someone had kicked out the plug to my stereo.

Side Two opens with "Here Comes the Sun," the best good-morning song since cornflakes were invented. George handles the frequent and tricky time changes

In 1969 I made a pilgrimage to the Apple offices in London (left) and to the place where it all started, the Cavern Club in Liverpool (above and opposite).

with a master's ease, fleshing out his already resonant vocal with a trumpetlike Moog synthesizer track and some precise three-part harmony. When he sings about it's being all right, we believe him. It is such a refreshing breeze after his earlier, darker pieces. NBC used "Here Comes the Sun" during its coverage of a total eclipse. Just as the sun's disk started to creep out from behind the shadow, the bright strains of the song were heard, as if God had choreographed the celestial happening to fit George's music.

I could do without "Because" and its breathy companion piece "Sun King." Short as they are, they are boring and tend to interrupt the flow of the album, although I do like the feeling that "Sun King" gives me of floating down a moonlit canal in a gondola. Paul picks things right back up, though, with his sarcastic "You Never Give Me Your Money." The lyrics emerged from the unhappy financial hassles at Apple: "And in the middle of negotiations you break down." The song takes two or three Lennonesque twists before escaping from the unhappy adult world of business into a childlike world where dreams come true and "all good children go to heaven."

The fake Italian-cum-Spanish-cum-English ("Cuesto obrigado tanta mucho que can eat it carousel" indeed) is rudely interrupted by the next song as if the Beatles

knew that "Sun King" was getting absolutely nowhere musically. "Mean Mr. Mustard" starts off like somebody's drunken uncle bashing open a door and stopping all conversation. He is certainly an unpleasant man to know ("sleeps in the park,/shaves in the dark"), one given to shouting out obscene things to Her Majesty. It's a portrait by Lennon worthy of Paul's musical paintbrush. Mr. Mustard's sister, "Polythene Pam," is a little better off, dressed to kill and making headlines in the *News of the World* with her attractive build. I love the snooty "yeah yeah" refrain, which bears no resemblance to the same words shouted six years earlier in "She Loves You."

The helter-skelter keeps turning, and we slide down into "She Came in Through the Bathroom Window." I think these are McCartney's oddest, most obscure lyrics ever. The song has terrific motion, but I don't understand anything of the images. "Golden Slumbers" was inspired by an old chestnut of a song Paul saw sitting on his father's piano one day, with lyrics by Thomas Dekker, a Shakespearean contemporary, who wrote them as follows:

Golden slumbers kiss your eyes;
Smiles awake you when you rise.
Sleep pretty wantons, do not cry,
And I will sing a lullaby.
Rock them, rock them, lullaby.

And rock us Paul does. I'd like to see someone try to

sleep through it. His rough-edged vocal is a little wrong for the song, but the string part is enchanting. After a brief burst from a thousand-voice choir singing "Carry That Weight," there is a quick snatch of a guitar riff and a reprise of "You Never Give Me Your Money," then, following a startling change in rhythm, back to "Carry That Weight."

We jump from there to the most virtuoso performance of their career by all four Beatles. "The End" lets us hear Ringo in his only real drum solo on a Beatles album, fifteen seconds of exhilarating rhythms and subrhythms. It always makes me wish he had done more like it. Then Paul, George, and John try to outplay each other on lead guitar, wailing away to their best abilities. If you listen you can tell who's playing what: Harrison's part is typically open and round-sounding, McCartney's high and pulsating, and Lennon's more rhythm-oriented than melodical. The guitars are swallowed up by a persistent piano triad and the gracious finale, which concludes with an orchestrated version of a riff from "You Never Give Me Your Money." We're left with the "amen" feeling for seventeen seconds, at the end of which Paul sings his chummy tribute to the queen.

Thank you, Beatles, for *Abbey Road.*

A radio promoter in Ohio is credited, if that word can be used, with touching off the most bizarre incident in the Beatles' history. The first inkling I had of it was in a letter from my sister, away at school in Lawrence, Kansas. She wrote commenting on my

After his marriage to Linda, Paul retreated to a farm in Scotland. His invisibility led to a bizarre rumor that he was dead, replaced by a look-alike. (Opposite) Sensationalism spread the hoax.

record album, saying some of the compositions "were almost as good as John Lennon's. I would have said 'Paul McCartney,' but he's dead."

Dead?

I was shocked; my heart raced. I hadn't heard. I immediately called KUDL.

"Nope," said a DJ. "Haven't heard a thing on that one." The next day I had just stepped out of the shower when the phone rang. It was Mary Lee Wilson, calling with the "news" of Paul's death and the series of clues that supposedly led to the inevitable, fatal conclusion. Theoretically Paul was supposed to have been killed in a car wreck in 1965. A "Paul McCartney Look-Alike Contest" was held, but the winner's name was never announced. That person was substituted for McCartney, and the world was none the wiser.

(The most grotesque item in my collection of Beatles memorabilia is a one-shot magazine called *Paul Mc-Cartney DEAD*. The back of the cover has a picture of the Beatles—including Paul (or his double)—and a legend reading: "We did it because we loved him." It is a supreme monument to bad taste and includes a montage of pictures captioned: "When did his double take his place?")

Anyway, I stood talking to Mary Lee on the phone, stark naked and dripping wet, listening to her recount a trail of "evidence" that Sherlock Holmes would have been proud to discover. After we hung up, I started digging out clues of my own. Some of them, dating back to 1965, are as follows:

Help!: Inside the fold-out cover, Paul is shown as the only one not wearing a hat.

Rubber Soul: "I'm looking through you, you're not the same." ("I'm Looking Through You")

—"with lovers and friends I still can recall,/some are dead . . ." ("In My Life")

Yesterday and Today: The cover, with its theme of death, was censored, then "covered up." On the new cover, Paul is sitting in a coffin-like trunk.

—"I'm not half the man I used to be" ("Yesterday")

Revolver: Paul is the only one drawn in profile, showing just one eye.

—"I was alone, I took a ride,/I didn't know what I would find there" ("Got to Get You into My Life")

Sgt. Pepper: On the cover, Paul is standing under an upraised hand, a sign of benediction.

—He holds an oboe, the only one of the instruments shown not found in a marching band.

—The Beatles are standing in front of an open grave.

—If Paul bent down to pick up the guitar made out of flowers, it would be a left-handed (but only three-

116

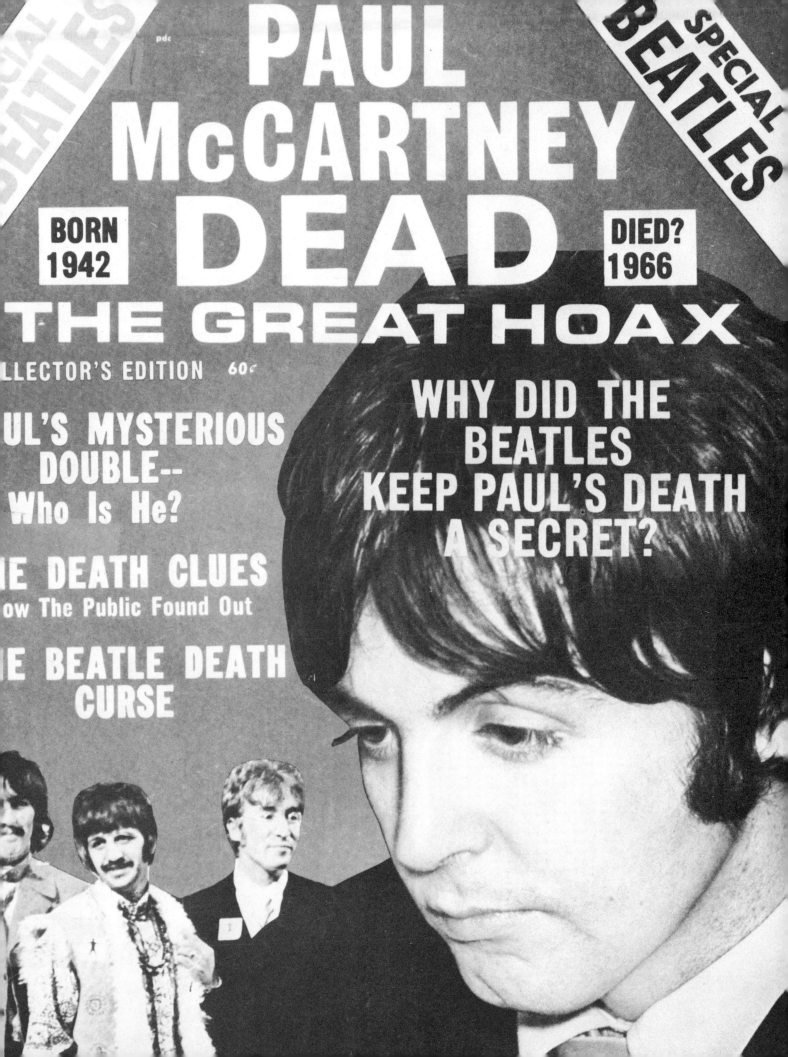

stringed) bass.

—It appears that the small doll in the green dress is looking at a toy car plummeting in flames over a cliff.

—Inside the sleeve, Paul is seated in the position associated with the burial of the dead in India.

—He wears a patch with the letters "O.P.D." which could stand for "officially pronounced dead."

—On the back, Paul has his back turned to us.

—On the back, George's hands form an "L," John's a "V" and Ringo's an "E." Paul's contribution is missing, but an "O" can be seen as one of the buttons on his sash.

—"He blew his mind out in a car" ("A Day in the Life")

Magical Mystery Tour: On the cover George the Rabbit's hand is raised (almost) above Paul the Hippopotamus's head.

—In the picture book, on page 3, Paul is seated at a desk behind a sign reading, "I Was."

—Paul is barefoot on pages 10 and 13; page 13 shows

The death rumor sent fans scrambling to the albums to pick out "clues" which supposedly told the whole tale. Paul came out of hiding to squelch the story in Life *magazine. (Below) I formed a group,* Mask; *all the members were very much alive.*

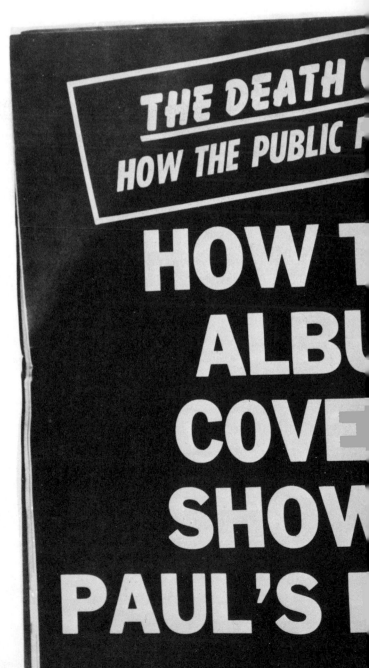

THE DEATH
HOW THE PUBLIC

HOW T
ALBU
COVE
SHOW
PAUL'S

his shoes next to Ringo's drums, on which is written a small *3*—three Beatles?

—On page 18 Paul again stands under an upraised hand.

—On page 23 he wears a black carnation; the others wear red.

—And again, on page 24, an upraised hand above his head.

—"The Magical Mystery Tour is dying to take you away" ("Magical Mystery Tour")

—"Nothing is real" ("Strawberry Fields Forever")

—"I buried Paul" ("Strawberry Fields Forever")

The Beatles: Ringo sings about someone who was in a car crash and who lost his hair. ("Don't Pass Me By")

—"Everybody's got something to hide. . . ."

—"Here's another clue for you all/The Walrus was Paul." ("Glass Onion") The walrus is supposedly a death symbol in Scandinavia.

—"Revolution # 9" has many buried references to death and dying, and "Number nine . . . number nine . . ." played backwards sounds shockingly like "Turn me on dead man . . . turn me on dead man." It does, I swear it.

Abbey Road: On the cover Paul is again barefoot and walks out of step with the others.

—He carries his cigarette in his right hand, odd for a southpaw.

—John is dressed as an angel in white, Ringo as a minister, Paul the way a corpse would be in Italy, George as a gravedigger.

—The license plate on the Volkswagen reads "28 IF," interpreted by the faithful as Paul's age "if he had lived."

—On the back of the jacket there is a crack running through the world "Beatles," symbolizing a "flaw in the structure."

—There is a chip in the "O" in "Road." Paul is the only Beatle without an "O" in his name; he also fails to provide the missing "O" in LOVE on the back of *Sgt. Pepper.* Is Paul now a "zero," an "O" missing from the love of the group?

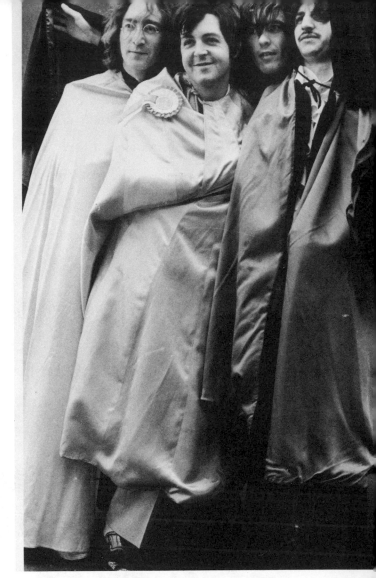

More from the Goldblatt series, taken about the time the Beatles began their final projects.

—"One and one and one is three" ("Come Together")
—"You can feel his disease" ("Come Together")
—"Got to be goodlooking 'cos he's so hard to see" ("Come Together")

Creepy, huh?

Of course the Beatles had explanations for everything. The lyrics all have dozens of possible interpretations. The Beatles themselves, the "old Beatles," are being buried in the Sgt. Pepper grave. "O. P. D." stands for "Ottawa Police Department," from whom they got the badge. "A Day in the Life" refers to a friend of theirs who was killed. As for the black carnation, "We ran out of red ones," said John. "Number nine" was from a tape John found in the studio of an EMI engineer announcing, "This is EMI test tape number nine"; any other sounds are purely coincidental. Paul's age was twenty-seven, not twenty-eight, when *Abbey Road* was released, and it's "cranberry sauce," not "I buried Paul".

I called KUDL again after I'd assembled all the clues, to inform them of the situation, since they didn't seem to know. The man on the phone said, "Hold on a second . . . okay, read those clues again." He was re-cording me, and the next day I heard a DJ parrot back a word-for-word transcription of my phone call on his program.

The Paul-is-dead school believed there was a phone number discernible in the structure of letters in the word "Beatles" on the cover of *Magical Mystery Tour*. Upside down the B looks like an 8, the E like a 3, the A like a 4, and so on. On page six of the book you can barely make out the number 834 on the blackboard behind John as the mustachioed ticket man. KUDL "deciphered" the whole number and called London on a Wednesday morning at five o'clock, the time referred to in the lyric line from "She's Leaving Home" that George is pointing to on the back cover of *Sgt. Pepper*. The number was that of an older-sounding man who, when asked to identify himself, said "PMC, is that enough?" (Paul *Mc*Cartney?) KUDL asked if he might have any information to give them. "Of what sort?" he asked. "Well, about the Beatles," said the DJ, not wanting to give anything away. "About the Beatles . . ." mused the Englishman. "I don't have anything for you right now. Perhaps you could call back tomorrow; say at nine o'clock?" (Nine o'clock is the other hour mentioned in "She's Leaving Home.") KUDL really played up the return phone call, and did it live on the air. The eerie thing was that when they called the number back, it had been mysteriously disconnected.

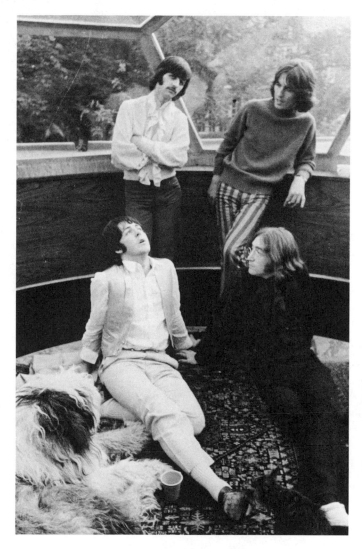

The radio stations were playing Beatles music constantly, making little attempt to squelch the story. It was drawing listeners and selling records, after all. One night, however, Walter Cronkite announced there was no truth to the rumor, and *Life* magazine proclaimed on its cover, "Paul Is Still With Us." Ringo summed it all up best: "It's a load of old rubbish."

At this time I was working with a band I called "Mask," and we played for a local theater group's awards banquet. Our drummer took off his shoes and we made a marching entrance, with him out of step and carrying a cigarette in his left hand (he was right-handed). As we set up to play we announced that "our drummer has been dead since 1947, so playing for you tonight is the winner of his look-alike contest."

My good friend Rick Enlow was also in Mask as its rhythm guitarist. He and I took a spontaneous jaunt to St. Louis one weekend where we stayed with people in a college dorm. We were still awake at four in the morning, chatting away and munching from little boxes of Kellogg's cereals. Suddenly Rick shoved some of the cereal under his rear end. "Look!" he cried, quoting from "I Am The Walrus," "I'm sitting on a cornflake!"

I tried it, too. "It's not very comfortable," I muttered, following suit. "Is the van here yet?"

John Lennon closed his prolific year with the release of the exquisitely painful and intensely, hypnotically primal "Cold Turkey." His *Wedding Album* finally came out, as did a record of some rock 'n' roll tunes called *Live Peace in Toronto 1969*, which would be okay if it weren't for Yoko's caterwauling on Side Two. Lennon had released three albums, two singles, and one biographical "Beatles" number—not a bad track record, although the quality was not uniformly good. He was constantly active in his advertising campaign for peace. One of his more charming stunts (or "events" as he and Yoko called them) was the sending of two acorns in a little bag to fifty heads of state. He also took out full-page ads in *The New York Times* and the *Times* of London, reading, in letters four inches high, "*WAR IS OVER* if you want it. Happy Xmas from John and Yoko Lennon." John also returned his MBE in protest over the war in Biafra, an event which irked more people than his accepting it had done.

I took delight in some of John's antics. He could still produce good music when he wanted to ("Cold Turkey" is painful proof). Anyway, the Beatles were almost like demigods—they had shown us before and they reconfirmed it with *Abbey Road*. Paul had even been resurrected from the dead. What more could anyone ask?

Immortality, that's what—something the Beatles as a group *didn't* have.

1970-1975

*. . . when across our universe the stars grew dark
and clouds drifted through our minds . . .
when fires flared and sleepers stirred
and love came again to brighten four dark corners . . .*

The breakup of the Beatles—or, if not the breakup, then the ultimate disappearance—was as inevitable as it was unfortunate. Popular culture thrives on its very expendability; the new must constantly rejuvenate, replenish, and replace the old. The Beatles, while they hadn't actually worn out their welcome, had absorbed all they could from the structure of the group. They were grown men now, each with wives, each with a head bursting full of musical ideas, with which the old

The Beatles and me, just before our graduations: mine from high school, theirs from each other.

structure was no longer able to cope. The time had come, the Walrus said, to talk of many things: of love and peace and families, of doing our own things.

In early 1970 I was carrying around a small pocket notebook my father had given to record my expenses.

On a whim I began listing in it any reference to the Beatles that happened to crop up during the day. Seen in retrospect, this brief diary captures a sense both of the Beatles' historical prominence and of their impending demise. Some of the entries:

Saturday, January 24, 1970: John & Yoko make front page by cutting their hair for peace and announcing 1970 is "Year One."

Tues., Jan. 27: Beatles mentioned in *Saturday Review* editorial.

Thurs., Jan. 29: *Abbey Road* receives honorable mention as best album of the year, 1969, *Time* magazine.

Friday, Jan. 30: "Bubble gum music is like the early Beatles"—*Life* mag.

Monday, Feb. 2: *Look* capsule of the 1960s bears caption, "I Read the News Today, Oh Boy. . . ."

Mon., Feb. 9: *Abbey Road*—Grammy nominee.

Tues., Feb. 10: *Look* mentions Ringo's appearance in *Magic Christian.*

Mon., Feb. 16: Paul McCartney voted best bass player, John and Paul best songwriters, in Playboy Poll. Beatles voted into Playboy Hall of Fame.

Mon., Feb. 23: Ringo appears on *Laugh-In.*

Tues., Feb. 24: *Hey Jude* album released.

Sunday, Mar. 1: Ed Sullivan show dedicated completely to Beatles.

Monday, Mar. 2: "Let It Be" on radio for first time in KC.

Wed., Mar. 4: Editorial in *KC Star* deals with mystic phenomena, quotes Lennon as an authority.

Sat., Mar. 7: Total eclipse broadcast on NBC; "Here Comes the Sun" played as the finale.

Fri., Mar. 13: "Instant Karma" hits #1; "Let It Be" enters the top 10.

Besides the proliferation of Beatle news articles and their daily exposure on radio (I heard four or five Beatles oldies a day), there was a stream of solo products like never before. Ringo opened in *The Magic Christian*, a wicked, appallingly tasteless film, in which he had a small tacked-on role. (John and Yoko were seen briefly, boarding the ocean liner.) Yoko's book of

poems, *Grapefruit*, was published, with an introduction by her husband ("Hi! My name is John Lennon. I'd like you to meet Yoko Ono"). Lennon was also running into trouble with his series of erotic lithographs, which caused a museum to close its doors for two days while the drawings were removed for "judicial appraisal." (Later they were declared "not obscene" and returned to the museum, although hung in a less conspicuous spot.) Paul's "Come and Get It," recorded by a Beatleish group called Badfinger, became a big hit, as was John's "Instant Karma."

And in early March, the single "Let It Be" was issued.

Beatleologists love to pounce on the ironic nature of the title when it is juxtaposed against Paul's announcement on April 10 that he was leaving the Beatles. It was a shock, but it was no surprise; all their music of the past twenty months indicated such a step was in the offing. I was totally confused by all the business and legal hassles, and still am. Other books document the court cases and countersuits much better than I can. Basically, though, the immediate issue centered on a controversy over release dates. Paul insisted his first solo album come out at a time that the other Beatles thought would conflict with the appearance of *Let It Be*. Paul, perhaps too stubbornly, insisted that *Let It Be* was never going to come out. That was a fair point; it had been in the can for a year while contract

and production problems were being ironed out. (As if to minimize the sadness and the fighting going on, Apple issued announcements that the delay was due to problems with the cover art.) As a Beatle fan, I saw no conflict of interest in a double release date. It just meant I would get two new albums instead of only one.

Paul *did* seem to be unnecessarily vehement, especially when he threatened to "finish off" Ringo, the emissary who had gone to explain things to him. But I see his anger as more symbolic than real. Here was his chance to break away, and he took it. After all, the four of them had released solo work before—Paul's *Family Way*, George's *Wonderwall*, Lennon's barrage of albums, and most recently Ringo's harmless *Sentimental Journey*. McCartney took a step the others wanted to take but never really did, at least as far as the public was aware.

On the day the Beatles' obituary appeared in the paper I wore an appropriate black shirt and black trousers to school. I even asked for a minute's silence in my English class. At the time I was part of a very close-knit group of friends that called itself "The Family." My "wife" made me an armband to wear as a symbol of mourning. (She was one of Simon and Garfunkel's most ardent fans. I bought her the *Bridge over Troubled Water* album for her birthday, "but only," I declared, "under protest.") I was scheduled to play two original compositions for the talent show, and for a

GEORGE HARRISON
ALL THINGS MUST PASS

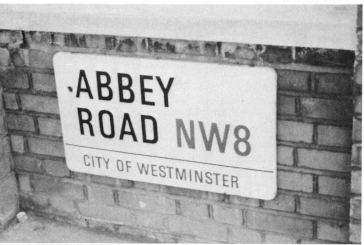

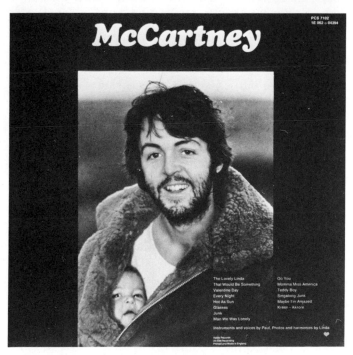

I couldn't locate the crossing shown on the Abbey Road cover (opposite), so I snapped one of the few remaining street signs (above center). 1970 brought us George's and Paul's first solo LPs.

while I considered switching one to a Beatle song as a farewell tribute. But there was a girl I loved to whom I had already dedicated the pieces, and I wanted her to hear them. I announced them as being "To Suzi, if she's listening." She wasn't; she hadn't even come to school that day.

Let It Be hit the stands the first week of May 1970. I was calling record stores daily to make sure I'd get a "first day" release. The record sold for $6.98—a big bite out of my limited income, but I didn't want to wait for a discount sale, which could take months.

The record is a sad one. There is no energy apparent anywhere, in the vocals, in the playing, or in the production. Some of the worst songs ever fill out the record. "I Dig a Pony" and "I've Got a Feeling" are slovenly and slipshod, their lyrics achingly obnoxious, their tunes spiritless and uninspired. Normally I would have chosen "Two of Us" as my favorite song, but it is mechanical and dull, dull, dull. George shines, but it is a hollow achievement; anyone can stand out when placed in front of a painted backdrop. "I Me Mine," his mournful counter to "You Never Give Me Your Money," waltzes along gracefully until interrupted by a rocking 4/4 section made even more exciting by Billy Preston's ripping organ track. The light, playful "For You Blue" skiffles happily to John's bottleneck and George's "Go, Johnny, go!" ad-libs.

But the heavy hand of wonder boy Phil Spector crushes the life out of "Let It Be," here remixed with a traffic-jam horn section. "The Long and Winding Road" fares even worse; a powdery-sugary choir carries our boys away to heaven on the wings of a magic harp. Bleah. I had to endure this one on the radio when Allen Klein shoved it out as an unwilling single. It wants to die, I said to myself, let it be. The studio bits found on the album are all coy and cute. "The queen says no to pot-smoking FBI members," quips John. "It's getting too cold to play chords," someone says in a snippet from the rooftop session. Warming up for "Get Back," John ad-libs some new, typically Lennonese, lyrics: "Sweet Loretta Fat, she thought she was a cleaner, but she was a frying pan." But it is all stale, all blown away. This album is no damn fun at all. If this is what the Beatles were producing, it's just as well they packed it in when they did.

I carried the album around school the next day, as if I felt a personal responsibility for promoting it. Some classmates and I were listening to it during a slack moment in progress on our government class final project, when the principal of the school walked in and announced that I had been chosen as one of two student speakers at the upcoming graduation ceremonies.

Graduation was a fiasco. My "family" of friends had taken a postschool, precommencement trip to the Lake of the Ozarks, where I fried like a fritter under the June sun. I broke out in sunburn blisters the size of nickels, which my sister carefully concealed with some of her makeup just before the ceremony started. It rained, of course, and we had to move inside. The other speaker and I took our places at the head of the rows and trooped into the auditorium. I gave my rather traditional speech first, using the opportunity to work in a reference to the Beatles: "We can no longer say, I'll wait until tomorrow. *Tomorrow never knows*; tomorrow never comes." Instead of sadness over leaving school, I felt anger: anger because I knew I'd never see most of those people again and that I would miss them terribly, terribly much; anger, too, that despite creative and scholastic success, I'd failed miserably to find meaningful, mutual love. I marched out of the auditorium with tears of frustration and loss burning my eyes.

My family (the real one—father-and-mother kind) and I spent three weeks traveling through Europe that summer. I expanded my record collection once again, this time absorbing all the English albums from *Please Please Me* to *A Collection of Beatles Oldies*. I also bought three copies of *Let It Be* to give away as gifts. These were special, because the English version was a boxed set containing the album and a marvelous thick book of pictures and transcriptions of dialogue from the movie. They made my suitcase weigh a ton, but it was worth it.

Let It Be, the film, was playing in Piccadilly Circus, advertised by the biggest poster I have ever seen. My brother Robert and I went to see it, but it left us feeling a little depressed. It was so sad to see the Beatles, my friends, bored and unhappy and bickering at one another. Poor John looks as though he wishes he were a million light-years away from there. George gets angry with Paul for telling him what to do, and as if to make matters worse, his microphone gives him an electrical shock. (George seems to have trouble with that sort of thing: he gets zapped in *Yellow Submarine*, and had to stand farther back from the microphone during the Bangla Desh concert because it kept snarling at him.)

John's first all-original, all-music solo album (below) drew raves from critics for its painful frankness and artistic self-revelation.

Ringo sits back, barely saying a word. The part of the film made during the rooftop concert, though, is worth enduring the rest of it. The Beatles are fond of saying that the film shows them with all their warts. I think I'd rather not have known.

Robert and I trucked from the theater to Apple, three blocks away. A black flag hung in front of the office. It struck me as a banner of mourning, but when a tiny breeze nudged its way into the narrow street and lifted the skirt of the flag, I could glimpse a bright green apple. Most of *Let It Be* was filmed in (and on top of) 3 Savile Row, and we got a charge out of touching the huge gold doorknob on the heavy white door that the Beatles had passed through so many times. As before, no Beatles were there, but Mal Evans, the amiable-looking roadie who had been with them since the Cavern days, walked through the lobby. The secretary—a different one from the year before—politely told me what all the Beatles were up to. As she gave me a publicity poster, I noticed her watch—a square one made of gold, with a green apple on the face. "Not for sale," she said, smiling. Two scruffy types ran in demanding to know whose car that was outside. "It's John's," the secretary said, "but he's just loaned it to somebody. He's away on holiday at the moment." Later I took the subway to Abbey Road, N.W. 1 to try to find the zebra crossing photographed on the *Abbey Road* album cover. All the street tiles had been torn off the walls for souvenirs by zealous fans. I walked for a mile in either direction but couldn't find "the" crossing. I snapped a few slides of a similar-looking one and left, disappointed.

While the Beatles went their ways, I went mine—to Los Angeles, to study film at the University of Southern California. I was without a car the first year, so the city seemed remote and a little hostile. The dorm was like a monkey house at feeding time. Sometimes, though, I found relief from the asphyxiating loneliness by closing the door, drawing the curtains, and listening to my treasured Beatles albums. I used to do what I called "hand dances" to "Within You Without You," while incense burned and candles flickered. About this time I discovered that "Hey Jude," played at ear-ringing volume through the headphones, was better than steak on Sundays and got me more ready for a philosophy test than did a week of studying.

I still bought the ex-Beatles' new albums, more out of habit, really, than out of a genuine desire to hear the music. I also made it a hobby to collect all the Apple releases, just for the heck of it. The problem was that Apple released some boring, and some just plain bad, music. Yoko started doing solo records, which purified John's albums a little but tarnished my own collection. Allen Klein released a couple of sound tracks on the label of films he'd produced, but when I realized I'd never played the second side of an obscure celluloid stinker called *Come Together*, it was time to quit. Apple has folded completely now, as symbolized by a tiny, half-eaten, wormy core printed on the back of George's last Apple album. The symbol of the Beatles' ideal hopes for the Seventies rotted away like an overripe, unwanted winesap.

Any further history of the Beatles must be told as four separate stories. We begin with

John

For some time, Lennon had taken an active part in helping Yoko tap another vein of her diverse, if controversial, talents, that of film-making. I got to see a few of her creations while in Los Angeles. One of them, an intriguing idea for a film, was *Rape*, in which they followed a poor, uncomprehending girl around Amsterdam for three solid days. They waited for her at her doorstep, caught up with her when she tried to run,

and never once told her what was going on. It was rape in the most cerebral sense. Another quaint concept was *Smile*. Yoko originally planned to make a movie "which included a smiling face snap of every single human in the world. But that had obvious technical difficulties." She scaled the project down to a ninety-minute slow-motion film (sets by "Garden," lighting by "God") of John's beaming face, "available for people who'd like to have the film on their wall as a light-

portrait." Her magnum opus, *Fly*, twenty minutes of the nasty little things crawling over a nude girl's body, won an ovation at the Cannes festival.

The Lennons underwent Arthur Janov's primal scream therapy in 1969; one result was the incredible "Cold Turkey," another was John's first "real" solo album, *John Lennon/Plastic Ono Band*. It's not a pleasant album to endure. The tone of the whole thing is expressed in that deathly pale apple on the label. Personal, painful, and sometimes ugly, *Plastic Ono Band*, often considered one of the top post-Beatle releases, delves into the unhappy parts of John's past and sets them to sparse, beat-heavy music.

It's one thing to be open and honest, it's another to communicate through objectivity. I find an impersonal "And I Love Her" is infinitely more expressive than, say, "Hold On John." Somehow when I know to whom a song refers, I can no longer relate to it as easily. "Eleanor Rigby" tells me more about the loneliness *I* feel, because I can make it *my* loneliness, than does "Isolation," which is only about *John's* loneliness. As one who thinks of John as a friend, I want to share his pain; as a listener to music, I want to find *myself* in the album too, but John's militant first-personism precludes doing so.

About this time I bought a puppy as a Christmas present for Suzi, who said she always thought of me whenever she heard "Something." I couldn't decide on a proper name for the thing until one day I fed him and

watched his belly swell to twice its normal size. Teasing him, I said, "You're a fat little . . ." and the word "budgie" popped into my mind from somewhere. Later I realized that the term came from one of Lennon's *Spaniard in the Works* poems, "The Fat Budgie":

> I have a little budgie
> He is my very pal
> I take him walks in Britain
> I hope I always shall. . . .
>
> He's on a diet now you know
> From eating far too much
> They say if he gets fatter
> He'll have to wear a crutch. . . .

And henceforth and hereafter all four-footed canines who pass strict requirements of cuteness, lovableness, and playfulness shall evermore be known to me as MBEs—Members of the Budgie Empire, or budgies for short. (Some people will try to tell you that budgies are birds, but don't you believe them.)

John, never one to shy away from the press, gave an interview to *Rolling Stone* which spread over two issues and nineteen huge pages. (In wonderful counterpoint to the interview, the same issues also carry an ad for *John Lennon/Plastic Ono Band,* a review of George's first solo album *All Things Must Pass,* a full-page "Happy Christmas" message from Paul and Linda McCartney in Halloween getup, and an ad for Badfinger's *No Dice,* with ghostly images of the Beatles appearing on various parts of a nearly naked girl. The ad rekindled rumors that Badfinger was just a reincarnation of the Beatles.) The interview itself, all thirty thousand words of it, drips with bitterness. John is so anxious to cast off the past that he belligerently insists he can't remember what song appeared on what album, or which album came before another. It's a little sad that the musical events which gave John his audience mean so little to him. But the man said what he believed, and it is a remarkable document because of it.

Just when it looked as though John was going to get it together, he released a single, "Power to the People," in March 1971. It's a silly piece, with garbled lyrics and a ridiculous picture of him and Yoko in Japanese riot helmets on the cover. It rode to number seven on the charts, don't ask me how.

The post-Beatles brouhaha climaxed when John recorded what for my money is his best work, *Imagine.* The excitement centered on the vitriolic "How Do You Sleep," a calculated attack on Paul McCartney, which wonders aloud how Paul, living with "straights" and creating "Muzak," could live with his conscience. John says the song was an answer to a track on *Ram,* McCartney's second solo LP, where Paul sings "We believe that we can't be wrong." In an interview, Lennon, affecting a veddy proper London accent, said, "Well, I believe that he could possibly *be* wrong." Much of the album, though, is tender and loving, including a mov-

ing apology to Yoko, "Jealous Guy," a noble, self-searching "How?" and the altruistic "Imagine." Political repression gets its lumps in the searing "Give Me Some Truth" (or "Gimme Some Truth," depending whether you read the liner notes or the record label). *Imagine*, while perhaps not as revealing as *Plastic Ono Band*, to my mind stands superior because of the beauty of the music and the more universal appeal of the lyrics.

A single called "God Save Us," written by John and Yoko to earn money for the defense trial of a supposedly obscene magazine, *Oz*, was issued in the summer of 1971. I saw it advertised in *Rolling Stone*, but it was nowhere to be found in Kansas City. When I returned to school that fall, I pilgrimaged to Phil Spector Productions on the Sunset Strip to inquire about it. While the secretary there went to the back room, I admired the Gold Record awards for *All Things Must Pass*, *Plastic Ono Band*, and *Let It Be* on the walls of the office. The secretary returned and gave me promotional copies of the hard-to-find single. Side One was credited to Bill Elliot and Elastic Oz Band, but the flip, "Do the Oz," was Elastic Oz Band only. It is actually pure Lennon. And it is pure trash.

The biggest disaster of John's recording career was the charmless, double-disc tabloid *Some Time in New York City*. I asked Apple about it two weeks before it came out in August 1972, but they disavowed any knowledge of it. I can understand why. Lennon had transplanted himself to the Big Apple and was swept up in the world of politicos and world-shakers. The "pick-a-cause-any-cause" Lennons penned forgettable anthems for any movement that needed one. Tapes of "Luck of the Irish," a clever, heartfelt acoustic folk ballad, were circulated among a select ten radio stations for advance air play. But by the time the song made the album, it was ruined by flutes, violins, oppressive percussion, and Yoko's out-of-sync verses ("The world will be one big Blar-ar-ney Stone." Heavens to Betsy, Yoko). A single, the deplorable "Woman Is the Nigger of the World," graced the airwaves with controversy for a while. *Some Time*'s second album is comprised of two concert excerpts, including one sludge of a track called "Scumbag." Just so. *Some Time* flat out reeks. So bad was the album that no second pressings ever had to be made. It was cut from the catalog and disappeared faster than cockroaches in sunlight.

John reinstated himself in my eyes with the touching "Happy Xmas (War Is Over)" single, the only official Beatles record pressed in clear green plastic (although Taiwanese Beatle bootlegs are pressed in green, red, and blue). I bought eight copies to give away as presents. Even Yoko sounds good, backed by what seems to be a million children with sleigh bells in their hands. Phil Spector's production enhances the exhilarating joy of the song, which seems to climb higher and higher with each verse. Christmas isn't Christmas anymore unless I get to hear the record.

(Below) With Yoko's daughter Kyoko before the fight for custody began. (Opposite) The Lennons moved to New York, where they were caught up in a swirl of political and human-rights movements.

In early 1973 a marketing company in Ohio released an illegal four-record boxed set of assorted Beatle tracks called *Alpha to Omega*. Brian Epstein had vowed there would never be a repackaging of Beatles' material, but he hadn't reckoned on encountering wily American bootleggers. The songs, thrown together in no particular order, sound as though they were re-recorded from records, not from the master tapes, and are therefore of considerably lesser quality. But the repackage sold well. John and George were in the best position to do something about it. They decided against court action, although the records were distributed without authorization by the copyright holder. A faster way to cut off sales was to release the Beatles' own collection of "the best of." Harrison and Lennon hastily and almost arbitrarily chose the tracks that were released as an eight-sided series, *The Beatles 1962-1970*. The cover, one of the ideas discarded from the *Let It Be* project, shows two pictures of the Beatles on the steps of the EMI offices in the same pose but taken seven years apart. Compare the faces.

John's own album, *Mind Games*, appeared in November 1973. It's competent, reaching neither the sublime levels of *Imagine* nor the pits of *Some Time*. I especially like "Bring on the Lucie" and the boogie-based "Tight A$." One particularly odd bit is the "Nutopian National Anthem," a three-second silence that harks back to John and Yoko's halcyon days of 1969. A note on the inside sleeve urges everyone to join the conceptual country Nutopia and gives an address to send away to for information. I obediently did and got

(Top) John with Yoko in a rare live concert; (above) with friend May Pang; (opposite top) back with Yoko ("the separation didn't work out") and with a small friend at a political rally.

my letter back marked "Addressee Unknown." It figures.

Poor John was now at the height of the debacle over his deportation order from the United States. It's amazing that he could fight that and produce music at the same time. The whole stupid issue revolved around John's 1968 drug bust and subsequent guilty plea, the result of a campaign by a police officer to plant the offending weed in rock stars' apartments. (So intent was

the officer on doing so, said John, that he rushed into one musician's apartment and "found" marijuana in the tenant's bedroom. It was obviously planted, because the musician kept *his* supply in a glass jar on a table in the living room, which the booby bobby had overlooked in his "search.") John was ordered to quit the country, which would have forced him to leave his wife and abandon his fight to win custody of Kyoko, Yoko's daughter, from Tony Cox, Yoko's former mate. Further complications arose when Yoko was granted permanent resident status and John was not. The deportation order was unsuccessfully appealed; another suit followed, another appeal. Round and round we go. It became increasingly clear that drugs were not the issue; John's political activities were, however, including some that were only rumored, according to Jack Anderson, political columnist. Anderson revealed that memos from Senator Strom Thurmond were circulated to Attorney General John Mitchell just before Lennon's deportation problems began.

Other rumors had it that John and Yoko were splitting up. For a while she was in New York while he was in Los Angeles, stirring up a little bit of drunken devilment by showing up at the Troubadour nightclub with a Kotex taped onto his forehead. Things were somewhat smoother when he quit drinking, reconciled himself with Yoko ("The separation didn't work out") and recorded *Walls and Bridges*, a step in the right direction.

A bouncy little single culled from the record, "Whatever Gets You Thru the Night," features Elton John on

133

(Above) John's immigration fight ended happily when the U.S. government dropped its case against him and allowed him to stay in the country with Yoko.

keyboards and backup vocals. I thought this was significant. While I was at USC, one of the dormies brought Elton's stupendous *Tumbleweed Connection* into my room to hear. Hardly five seconds of the first song had played when I declared prophetically that this man would be to the Seventies what the Beatles were to the Sixties. Turns out I wasn't far wrong. And now the paths of the two had crossed, on *Walls and Bridges* and again on later recordings. So successful was John's album that another single, the gently beautiful "#9 Dream," was issued. Lennon humorously continued the "How Do You Sleep" business with his tacit introduction to the similar-sounding "Steel and Glass": "This is a song about your friend and mine. Who is it? Who is it?"

The year 1975 heard no new songs from Lennon. His album, *Rock 'n' Roll*, is a collection of jukebox standards from the Fifties, marvelously and authentically done. An interesting footnote is that John apparently gave permission to Adam VIII, an independent packaging label, to use the masters for an album called *Roots: John Lennon Sings the Greatest Rock and Roll Hits*. The records were pressed and the sleeve printed, but a court injunction instigated by Capitol, which claimed exclusive rights to the album, prevented its appearance in stores. It's a pity, because there are two songs on *Roots*, "Angel Baby" and "Be My Baby," that never appeared on *Rock 'n' Roll*. *Shaved Fish*, a record of Lennon's greatest hits, released at the end of the year,

contains four recordings not found on other albums but is marred by a rough "medley" which jams "Give Peace a Chance" and "Cold Turkey" into one track. Boo.

Lennon's fight to stay in the country was finally won in October 1975. Part of the defense was an accusation that Watergate tactics, specifically wiretapping, had been used under the direction of John Mitchell, then Attorney General. John (the Beatle) must have touched a sore spot because the government very quickly dropped the case after that. I did my part by writing to President Ford and asking that he intervene. I also wrote to my congressman, who surprised me by actually getting in touch with the right people on my behalf and forwarding all of his information on the case to me. When the announcement came that Lennon could remain in the country, I felt I had something to do with it. Yoko's pregnancy didn't hurt the cause any, either. On October 9, John's own birthday, the Lennons' first child was born. They originally planned to name him George Washington United States of America Citizen Lennon to demonstrate the extent of John's commitment to this country, but they settled for Sean.

John has said that he prefers being in the studio to doing concert tours. "I used to be alone a lot, so I was always either reading a book or writing or drawing. It was only music that pulled me out and got me in front of people on a stage—which turned out to be great, too, for a while. But writing and recording are the best.

"The artist's function," he went on, "is to be as true to himself, and therefore to the people he communicates with through his art, as he can. And survive."

Survive well, John.

Paul

It's not surprising that Paul was thought to be dead. He had a studio built in his home and did much of his work there. The Beatles hadn't appeared for years publicly. He thought it was time to end the charade.

Paul's solo album, *McCartney*, is the one that caused all the fuss. I like it a lot—it's unpretentious and spontaneous, with a more open feeling than some of John's overbearing wall-of-sound productions. "Maybe I'm Amazed" is one of the greatest tracks on any solo Beatles record. It was so popular in Kansas City it made the local charts without even being re-leased as a single! I first heard it on "The Ed Sullivan Show," where a film of Linda McCartney's slides was shown while the piece played in the background. "Every Night" is exceptionally good, and "Junk" is laden with concise, haunting images. "Oo You" is decent enough for having been just improvised in the studio. As good as the music is, the cover is a disaster. Inside are some of the grossest, most tasteless pictures ever immortalized on an album. The censored *Yesterday and Today* sleeve was a Rembrandt compared to some of Linda's ideas of cuteness. My biggest objection to the album, apart from the jacket photos, is Paul's

drumming. It wasn't good on "The Ballad of John and Yoko," and it isn't good here. But he tried.

The whole Beatles mess spilled into court at the end of 1970. McCartney filed a writ calling for a dissolution of "The Beatles Co.," charging that manager Klein was incompetent and that their bookkeeping affairs were a mess. The suit asked that partnership affairs be ended and the income of each partner be separated. The other three Beatles, named as codefendants, were represented by their own solicitors.

While the courts were humming with Beatle activity, Paul released a surprisingly calm and occasionally touching single, "Another Day." The authorship was credited to "Mr. & Mrs. Paul McCartney," an indication of the growing influence this Beatle spouse, like Yoko, was having over her mate.

Paul shocked a lot of people by appearing in person at the Hollywood Palladium to accept a Grammy for best motion-picture score of 1970, *Let It Be*. Black-tied cynics accused the tennis-shod McCartney of being sure he, not the others, picked up any Beatle awards. McCartney and his wife ducked through a crowd of photographers and reporters ("Are you here to cut a record?" "Yes, with a knife."), escaping into a Cadillac, and driving off among the shrieks and cheers of surprised fans. I was a little glad he stole the show from Simon and Garfunkel, who practically needed a truck to cart off their six Grammies for *Bridge Over Troubled Water*.

Paul told his side of the breakup story to *Life* magazine in April 1971. "I do think if it were just up to the four of us we would have picked up our bags—these are my shoes, that's my ball, that's your ball—and gone. And I still maintain that's the only way, to actually go and do that, no matter what things are involved on a business level. But of course we aren't four fellows. We are part of a big business machine. So that's why I've had to sue in courts to dissolve the Beatles, to do on a business level what we should have done on a four-fellows level. I feel it just has to come."

He says he searched his soul before he decided to go to court. "People said, 'It's a pity that such a nice thing had to end.' I think that too. It *is* a pity. I like fairy tales. But you realize that you're in real life, and you don't split up a beautiful thing with a beautiful thing."

Ram, Paul's second album, came out in the middle of May 1971. I remember I had just packed up all my belongings—except my stereo; I was saving that till last—to ship home after school let out. It was a hot day in Los Angeles, and I lay sweating on my bed staring at the bare, hollow, cinder-block walls of USC's Trojan Residence Hall, listening to the record. "Too Many People" is *Ram*'s high point for me. Unfortunately it's all downhill from there. I think it's sloppily made, just too many loose ends that go nowhere. "Uncle Albert/Admiral Halsey," a Noël Cowardian montage, was the number-seven song of the whole year 1971. Humph. "Smile Away" is fun, but "Monkberry Moon Delight" drones on to a singularly obnoxious vocal by Paul and flat, monotonous backups by Linda. "The Back Seat of My Car" is a dandy, complete with strings and a strong melody/lyric line. It's interesting now to hear the little snatch of a song just at the end of Side Two

that eventually became "Big Barn Bed" two albums later. The cover of *Ram* is another monstrosity. The photo of Paul grabbing the situation by the horns was satirized by Lennon, who did the same to a pig on a postcard stuck inside *Imagine*. (Later the card was changed to a harmless idyllic one, showing John as Pan with his pipes.) On the back of *Ram* is a lovely shot of two beetles fornicating—is there some significance there? You can read the initials "L.I.L.Y." on the front; the story has it that they stand for "Linda I love you."

McCartney created a permanent (well, almost) band called Wings, drawing on the talents of *Ram* drummer Denny Seiwell and a guitarist, Denny Laine. The debut LP, *Wild Life*, was rushed out by November. By now my roommate was a little disgusted by my Beatle devotion, especially in light of the rather inferior product we'd been getting of late. *Wild Life* did nothing to change his opinion of them or me. My favorite review of the album put it perfectly: "It's just a record." And it is. No greatness asked for, none had. That's good in one respect, but bad in another. Without striving there is no achieving. There are two nonsense songs on the record, one too many: "Mumbo," which Paul said was done in one improvised take, was said to be typical of what we could expect from Wings. Uh-oh, I cried. "Bip Bop" is unnecessary, as is a particularly long version of "Love Is Strange," the first non-Beatle-written recording since 1966. The second side is much better, with some very pleasant material. "Some People Never Know" does have a line about people being able to sleep because they believe love never dies, which should answer John's question. "Dear Friend" seems much more like a soft slap at Lennon: "Does it really mean so much to you?" The cover of *Wild Life* is the bare minimum and features the worst liner notes since

Paul and his wife Linda (opposite above) retreated to a secluded farm in Scotland (below and opposite) where they settled into a cozy domesticity that was reflected in their music.

Edison rediscovered sound.

Shortly after the release of Wings' first record the group took off in their bus for a trip across England. "We were traveling along the M-1 highway at the time and one of the group said he had fond memories of playing there, so we just made for Nottingham." Students at Nottingham University got a surprise, unannounced concert, Wings' first public appearance. The band ran out of rehearsed numbers, an experience Paul described as "unnerving." They continued doing shotgun appearances until they felt more ready for an official, promoted tour.

As if the legal and musical battles weren't enough, another argument flared up in early 1972 when Paul granted an interview to *Melody Maker*. "John and Yoko are not cool in what they're doing. . . . So what if I live with straights? I like straights. I have straight babies. It doesn't affect him. . . . If it wasn't for Klein I might have had second thoughts [about playing in George's Bangla Desh concert]. Allen's a good talker. The others really dig him, but I've made the mistake of

In 1971 Paul formed Wings, which included Linda and former Moody Blue Denny Laine (top). Their breezy, easy music, though irksome to critics, earned them a pile of gold (opposite top).

trying to advise them against him and that pissed them off. I think they might secretly feel that I am right, though." The article drew a scathing response from Lennon, who disclaimed that he, John, was the one blocking the settlement and blaming it on the "taxman." "Your conceit about Klein is incredible—you say we secretly feel that you're right! Good God! You must know *we're right about Eastman*. . . . No hard feelings to you either. I know basically we want the same, and whenever you want to meet, all you have to do is call."

In February 1972 Paul took a swing at the political situation in Britain with Wings' first single, "Give Ireland Back to the Irish." It just begged to be banned, and it was, an event already planned for on the B side of the record, which was a note-for-note instrumental version of the A side. English ads proudly read "New McCartney single BANNED EVERYWHERE," although the inoffensive nonvocal track could be broadcast. The song itself is far less exciting than the publicity surrounding it. Almost as if in answer to the

controversy Paul released a peculiarly distasteful little opus, "Mary Had a Little Lamb," which even McCartney disclaimed: "I don't get into it that heavy." The flip, "Little Woman Love," is a good piano-based rocker.

Paul and crew departed for a tour of Europe in June, and the first "official" Wings concert took place in France. Asked why he didn't kick off the tour in Britain or America, he said he'd rather polish the band in places that expected less from him than the Beatle-hungry English-speaking countries. He wanted to play to smaller houses than the Beatles had: "We don't have too many performance ambitions. The ambitions are all in the music."

In December, following a pair of drug busts, the McCartneys' song "Hi Hi Hi" was also banned by the BBC because of the line, "I want you to lie on the bed and get you ready for my body gun." Shame on you, Paul.

The signal that big things were about to happen came in March 1973 with the release of "My Love," a single

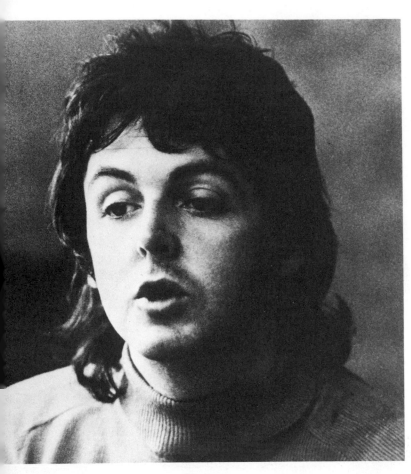

snipped from the *Red Rose Speedway* album. I first heard it through a transistor radio with reception that sounded like sandpaper on cement, but I could tell it was McCartney, and good McCartney at that. I was enrolled at Occidental College in Los Angeles at the time, having left the USC zoo at the end of my sophomore year. I was heavily involved in the drama department, but luckily I weaseled out of a rehearsal so I could go to the dorm and watch the "James Paul McCartney" TV special on April 3. The show was awfully bizarre, especially the "My Love" segment which had what must be the world's oldest group of violinists. Also odd was the "Gotta Sing, Gotta Dance" number in which a mustachioed Paul did a boring tap routine flanked by a chorus line of women made up on one side to look like men. The show ended with a heartrending acoustic solo version of "Yesterday," which made up for all the sins that went before. I wept like a two-year-old when I heard the song. I went to the piano to find some release and played Beatle songs for three straight hours.

Red Rose Speedway came out a month later, proving Paul had things back under his musical control. So much so, in fact, that the group was now called "Paul McCartney and Wings." There are some fine tunes on the album, including a rich-harmonied "Big Barn Bed," a delightful confection, "Little Lamb/Dragonfly," and an intricate, clever medley of four songs that stack up on one another like well-fitting china plates. There is an occasional dog, like "Loup" and "When the Night," but "Get on the Right Thing" more than adequately compensates. The cover was finally decent,

(Opposite) Baby-faced Paul brought Wings to New Orleans and the desert for Venus and Mars *publicity shots. (Top) Paul tests his terpsichorean talents in a bizarre April 1973 TV special; (above) the* Band on the Run *cover featured celebrities in a whimsically uncharacteristic pose.*

Although McCartney has established himself and his good-time band as a musical force to be reckoned with, his first priority, he says, is his wife and three daughters.

too, including the little message in Braille on the back, intended for Stevie Wonder: "We love you, baby."

Paul's most productive year yet rolled on with a second-rate theme for a third-rate James Bond flick, *Live and Let Die.* The sound-track album has only the one performance by McCartney; other tracks are competently handled by the brilliant George Martin. "Helen Wheels," Paul's third 1973 single, popped up in October. It's a decent piece, with an oddly remote vocal and some obscure (to Americans anyway) lyrics.

(In November the three composing Beatles, including Lennon, sued Allen Klein. Perhaps Paul was right after all.)

Decorating the end of 1973 like a string of Christmas lights was Paul's marvelous masterpiece, *Band on the Run.* Just before it was to have been recorded, two members of the group dropped out, but Paul, Linda, and Denny Laine bravely forged ahead at a Nigerian studio. Paul surprises me with his sterling drumming on this album (for a while I thought some one else *had* to be doing it). But even more exciting are the superb compositions.

Not one song on the entire creation is unworthy. "Jet" is a gas, a nonsensical but swift-moving stomper that generates a good deal of its energy from a tripleted lyric line set against a straight 4/4 beat. The lyrics show Paul's marvelous ability to put together words that sound fantastic. "Let Me Roll It" wryly but lovingly captures John Lennon's style of recording without mocking it in the least. The beautiful string arrangements on "No Words" and "Picasso's Last Words" are the best Paul has ever come up with. There's even a built-in encore, "Nineteen Hundred and Eighty-Five," which builds to a galvanized, synthesizer-dominated James Bond climax. One interesting footnote to the album is a controversy over the release of the "Jet" single. In England and elsewhere, the flip side is "Let Me Roll It." First issues of the single in America had that song, but on later ones the flip was switched to "Mamunia." Why?

The cover of *Band on the Run* is novel: surrounding Paul, Linda, and Denny are English broadcaster Michael Parkinson, singer Kenny Lynch, James Coburn (yup, that's Jim!), Clement Freud, grandson of Sigmund and member of Parliament, and Christopher Lee, actor.

"Junior's Farm," a single, came out in November 1974 but was an unsatisfying follow-up to *Band.* Actually it was the flip side, "Sally G," which got most of the attention, so much so that Capitol even released a promotional version of it to radio stations.

The press made much of McCartney's jaunt to New Orleans for the Mardi Gras, from which period emerged *Venus and Mars.* As a companion piece to *Band on the Run* it is disappointing; on its own terms it stands competently. "Listen to What the Man Said" is a fun thing, making better use of a saxophone than I've heard in a long time. "Love in Song" is a grippingly haunting tune, and "You Gave Me the Answer" is a charmer. The innocence of its line "I love you and you —you seem to like me" is the most effective understatement of love since Elton John's shy-boy "Your Song." It's a good album but one slightly less intriguing than its predecessor.

Wings' *At the Speed of Sound,* released to coincide with Paul's U.S. tour in May 1976, is a sincere attempt to spotlight the other members of the band but boasts little of the songwriting genius present in *Band on the Run.*

Paul places his wife and family at the top of his priority list, letting music ride in the back seat of his car. "Our children will always be our primary concern. It's a great pleasure—and a tough job—to raise children.

"Nothing is left of the Beatles now; only memories," he said. "My ambition now is just to be happy."

Be ever so, Paul.

George

George's years of composing songs in the shadows of Lennon and McCartney suddenly ended during the breakup in 1970. The result, like a flood of water from a bursting dam, was the colossal three-record set, *All Things Must Pass*. The title cut alone was at least two years old (George can be seen rehearsing it during the film of *Let It Be*), and the record as a whole shows what we had been missing. Phil Spector produced the basic tracks, but George handled all the overdubs. Splendidly, I might add.

The album is nearly perfect in all ways, although it tends to run out of steam toward the end. "My Sweet Lord" was the best-selling record of 1971 and was voted best song of all time in a questionable poll taken by a Los Angeles radio station. The song was the culmina-

tion of a movement in music known as "Jesus Rock," which included such works as "Jesus Christ Superstar," "Bridge Over Troubled Water," and "Spirit in the Sky." George was sued over "Lord's" musical proximity to "He's So Fine." What I find most amazing is that George sings every one of the harmonies on the song—on the whole album, in fact, cleverly credited to "The George O'Hara Smith Singers." His brilliance in arranging at last shines through, and it is rewarding. "What Is Life," also released as a single, is my favorite, a catchy and unpretentious little number. "Isn't It a Pity" does a nice job of parodying "Hey Jude," right down to its length (a scant *one second* short of "Jude's" mammoth 7:11). Listen to that chorus (George again) doing its thing in the fade-out, and you'll hear what I mean about a parody. The lyrics can be interpreted as a gentle chiding of McCartney's post-Beatle behavior.

Other gems include the unusual, endearing "Apple Scruffs," a song about the flower children who inhabited the steps of the Apple office trying to glimpse their heroes. It reveals a new talent of George's, a wonderfully airy and bright mouth-organ solo. Again, the backup vocals glisten like crystal. "Awaiting on You All" moves almost too quickly for George to spit out a strong set of lyrics, including one piercing line, unmentioned on the lyric sheet, "The pope owns fifty-one percent of General Motors; the stock exchange is the only thing he's qualified to quote us." I love the sinister rock feeling of "Art of Dying" and the peppery "It's Johnny's Birthday," a theme that sounds identical to a Cliff Richards song, "Congratulations." A free record called *Apple Jam* was included in the set and is enjoyable, if not outstanding, improvisational rock. It's a good chance for George to let down his (by then rather long) hair.

George's musical contribution to 1971 was one that made history on social, political, and economic levels

as well. His amazing Bangla Desh benefit concerts on the first day of August were announced by a very small but not overlooked ad in *The New York Times*, "George Harrison and Friends." Tickets were sold out twelve hours before the box office even opened because police had to insist the tickets be distributed to break up a traffic jam created by the swarms of fans already in line. I was in Grand Lake, Oklahoma, at the time, wondering if there was any way I could hop a quick plane to New York for the show. I had to be content with reading the newspaper reports, which stated that forty thousand people heard the two concerts. No one knew until the time of the shows just who would appear, and it was rumored that John Lennon had flown into New York for the weekend. The paper said the crowd was near hysteria when Ringo sang "It Don't Come Easy" and tossed his hair in acknowledgment of the applause.

It was hoped that the record of the concert could be

George showed his devotion to Krishna by penning the best-selling single of 1971, "My Sweet Lord," and by helping followers establish temples (opposite). The camera-shy Harrison created his own record label, Dark Horse, in 1974.

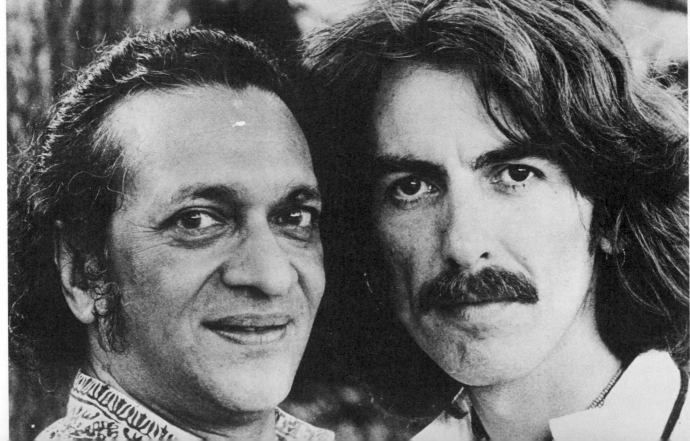

released within two weeks; George and Phil Spector set to work on the mix-down the very next day. There were delays and contractual problems, however, and the record barely made it out by Christmas 1971.

The album itself is miraculous. Dylan's full side of music is usually touted as the album's high point, but not being a Dylan fan, I prefer certain of the other cuts. Ravi Shankar's sitar duet with Ali Akbar Khan on sarod is a thrill, like hearing a debate between two brilliant minds. George, surrounded by twenty-six of rock's top instrumentalists and vocalists, bursts through with spirited versions of his most popular songs. Like a gentleman, he steps aside to allow his guests to take the floor: Billy Preston, with his soulful "That's the Way God Planned It"; Ringo with a fumbling, word-dropping version of "It Don't Come Easy" ("I couldn't read the words," he laments); and Leon Russell with a slick, almost sterile medley of rock numbers. Harrison's best effort is the simplest one: an acoustic "Here Comes the Sun," as delicate as the sunlight that permeates George's high, windy voice.

The concert earned $243,418 for the UNICEF fund for relief of refugee children. Sales of the "Bangla Desh" single and the concert album pushed the figure over the seven-million-dollar mark, and receipts from the film earned even more for the fund. For their efforts George Harrison and Ravi Shankar were honored with the "Child Is Father to the Man" award, given by the United Nations.

The film of the concert didn't come out until spring 1972. The project consumed so much of George's time that he released no new music that year. *Bangla Desh* on screen is all we could have expected and more. Despite the technical problems of blowing up 16mm to 70mm and of editing to fit an existing sound-track album, the movie retains a real feeling of freshness and atmosphere. Especially effective is the six-channel sound, which captures the presence of the instruments and the audience.

There were persistent rumors at the time that Allen Klein was deriving a little personal financial reward from the project. But George was keeping such a close eye on everything, from mixing the album to selecting film footage, that it seems unlikely any money intended for starving children found its way into Klein's hands.

It was almost eighteen months after the release of *Bangla Desh* before Harrison's next record was released, which meant there was a two-and-a-half-year gap between new material. It wasn't worth the wait, really. *Living in the Material World* is a generally depressing album, especially after the high-spirited optimism of his first two releases. I was studying for the final in my Shakespeare class at Occidental when my roommate bought the album and presented it to me as a gift. It didn't lighten my academic load any at the time, but it did provide some nice moments. "Don't Let Me Wait Too Long," a pale remake of "What Is Life," is one of the few up-tempo songs on the record. "Give Me Love," the single from the album, makes me feel like gasping for breath when George sings those long chanting *oms*. The title tune sounds as if it were recorded too slowly, but the beat moves along at a good trot, interrupted by two flute-dominated refrains in a

George's tour of the U.S. (opposite) was marred by his overworked voice, some unfamiliar material, an overly generous portion of esoteric Indian music by Shankar, and by what amounted to a nearly bitter denial of his Beatle heritage.

completely separate key that float up like perfumed air. "Be Here Now" is a beautifully weightless piece of gossamer that drifts in and out of the psyche like a voice in a dream. Well-produced, flawlessly performed, the album is unfortunately a little dull and drab.

By now the influence of Indian culture and religion had taken a solid hold on George. His music relied heavily on Eastern instrumentation and was heavy with spiritual significance. He produced an album for the Radha Krishna Temple, London, containing several surprisingly melodic mantras with just a touch of Western rock influence. In Paris George helped followers of Krishna find a suitable location for their temple. At USC a Krishna group staged one of their noisy, colorful celebrations. I sampled some of their holy foods but couldn't finish the cloyingly sweet fruits and breads. The campus security force insisted they move the festivities off campus, which annoyed me because certain other groups, political as well as religious, were allowed to inhabit the area with their pamphlets and proselytizers. Phooey. Injustice frustrates me.

The big musical event of 1974 was unveiled in the middle of summer when George announced his plans for a concert tour. He came to Los Angeles for four concerts, November 10-12. On the day tickets went on sale I raced to a box-office outlet an hour early. I was second in line, and knew I'd get a good seat. When the place finally opened, it was announced that its share of the tickets hadn't been received. Grr and piffle. I tore to another outlet, a computerized one, and soon had two $9.50 tickets for the evening of the twelfth in hand. After I'd lined up a date with a beautiful girl from school, there was nothing to do but wait.

We had dinner then drove to the L.A. Forum. The show was an hour late in starting, not atypical for a

George, always the shy and quite one, is as complex and elusive as his music. His deep faith and passionate concern for humanity have earned him the title "the gentleman of rock."

rock show. We passed the time reading the programs we bought, proceeds from which would go to aid Appalachian Regional Hospitals. Good ole George. When he finally made his entrance, wearing a high-crowned hat with a big pink feather, a banner was unrolled from the ceiling, on which was painted the prancing, seven-headed horse, symbol of George's newly found record label, Dark Horse. The concert was rather a bore, I'm sorry to say. "There's something missing," my girlfriend whispered, but we couldn't put our fingers on what it was. Poor George had been working so hard rehearsing the band, creating new material, recording a new album, that his voice was just shot. Also he allowed Ravi Shankar to present an overlong set of Indian music, causing the pace and the audience's enthusiasm to slacken. George almost poutingly refused to play the music he knew his audience would really like to hear. When he did grudgingly allow "While My Guitar Gently Weeps" to creep in, he changed the lyrics to "while my guitar tries to smile." Similar modifications were wreaked on "In My Life" ("In my life I've loved God more . . .") and "Something" ("When something's in the way, we move it . . .").

I was really glad I'd finally gotten to see a Beatle perform but sorry he hadn't done better. The concert was far from sold out, and was not very well received by the audience. His album *Dark Horse*, released during the tour, was a critical disaster. George's voice, hoarse and raspy, was now preserved forever on wax. I do enjoy "Hari's On Tour (Express)," a catchy instrumental, and the snappy "Ding Dong; Ding Dong." "Dark Horse" has some beautiful flute work in it but silly lyrics, and "It Is He (Jai Sri Krishna)" is a lovely, ingratiating little chant. It's certainly a happier record to hear than *Material World*, marred, however, by some ho-hum tunes and a self-indulgent version of "Bye Bye Love," rewritten to fit George's then-current marital situation.

It had been eighteen months between each of the last two albums; *Extra Texture* hit the stands a relatively short ten months after the release of *Dark Horse*. Under a remarkably good picture of a grinning Harrison on the inner sleeve is the cryptic legend, "OH-NOTHIMAGEN." George's face seems to be saying, "I know all you critics out there hoped I wouldn't be back for a while, but here I am. Oh, yes, me again." And we should rejoice.

Extra Texture is a flawless creation. There is much less stress on Indian mysticism, which chops about a pound of excess weight off right there. The songs are bright, well-conceived, and highly melodic. One is even damn funny, a tribute in nonsense verse to rock's omnipresent nonsense man, "Legs" Larry Smith. George's normally instructing, lecturing lyrics have given way for the most part to happy, tender sentiments of love. He completely subdues his own personality and speaks tenderly to an unnamed "you." It is a consistently rewarding album, rich in synthesizer effects and witty surprises. A job well done.

When asked at a news conference in the early Seventies what his ambitions were, George replied simply that he wanted to manifest the divinity that's in all of us. "My only ambition is to be God-conscious."

Bless you, George.

Ringo

Everyone feared for Ringo's future when the Beatles broke up. He had just released *Sentimental Journey*, a collection of old standards, that failed to stir much interest. In September 1970, however, he came closer to the mark with an album of country tunes, recorded in a two-day marathon session, called *Beaucoups of Blues*.

"I was a bit uptight and stiff at first," Ringo remembers. "I was singing straight, you know, and Pete Drake, the steel guitarist, said, 'Come on, get into it or I'm gonna come out there and stomp on your toes.' He made me cry, and then I sang 'em country." Ringo drew from his then-current "sad times" to find something to relate to on the album. The record, which is truly a good one of its genre, made it to the Top 30, though I'm afraid more on the basis of Ringo's name than on the wings of inspired talent.

In April 1971, Ringo released what I consider the best

single (as opposed to track lifted from an album) ever issued by a solo Beatle, "It Don't Come Easy." Ringo likes saying that it took years to write: a verse here and a verse there, whenever he felt inspired. Aided by George Harrison's uncanny ear for production and his silvery guitar solo, "Easy" is perfectly constructed and executed. It establishes Ringo as the proverbial talent to be reckoned with, and I'm proud of him for it. The flip side is a cute tribute to three unnamed men, one of whom "lives on a farm, got plenty of charm," another who lives with his wife, "she's Japanese," and the third, a "long-haired cross-legged guitar picker." I wonder who they could be. . . .

I didn't care so much for Ringo's next single, "Back Off Boogaloo," which came out in March 1972. (Footnote: The record came out on a blue (*gakk*) apple label in England; George's album had an orange apple, John's was white, Paul's third album had none at all.)

An excellent single, "Photograph," cowritten by Ringo and George, foreshadowed the release of the spectacular hit, *Ringo*. The big-nosed drummer had returned to the rock flock and brought along with him the other three Beatles, Harry Nilsson, The Band, David Bromberg, Marc Bolan, and so on and so on. His material was good ole pop-rock tunes, sprinkled with spicy production by Richard Perry and a "damn-it-we're-gonna-have-a-good-time-if-it-KILLS-us" attitude. The record was so successful that three singles were released from it. Klaus Voorman designed a thick, austere book to illustrate the lyrics. (Another footnote:

the tape cassette version of the *Ringo* album has about a minute of ad-libbed music by Paul McCartney, right at the end of "Six O'Clock," that does not appear on the record. Why?)

The follow-up album, *Goodnight Vienna*, was really more of a rehash of the old formula than a step in a new direction. Again, three singles from the record made the charts, most notably "Only You" and "No No Song." *Blast from Your Past*, Ringo's greatest-hits package, contains both of these songs but is the more valuable for having included "It Don't Come Easy."

Because all four Beatles appear on *Ringo* (but not all play on any one track) rumors of a reunion abounded. One person I talked to *swears* he saw all four Beatles in a Warner Bros. recording studio. Each Beatle, when asked to comment, has said basically the same thing: "We may get together and we may not. It all depends how we feel."

Ringo has continued his film career, from roles in *Candy* and *The Magic Christian* to *200 Motels, Blindman, Lisztomania*, and his biggest critical success, *That'll Be the Day*, a fictionalized biography of the rise of an English pop musician to stardom. Ringo played a worldly wise Teddy Boy carnival attendant who coached the musician on some of the more devious

(Below) Ringo snapped his own portrait at the birth of daughter Lee in 1970, but stayed in front of the cameras for roles in Blindman, Son of Dracula, *and* 200 Motels *(opposite)*.

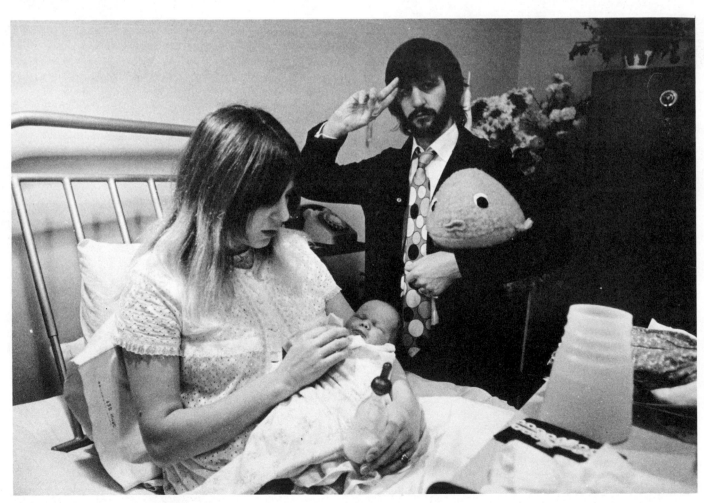

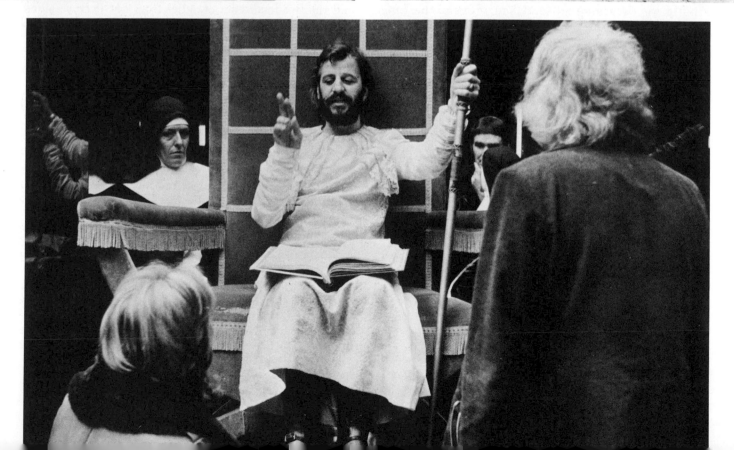

Ringo came closest to effecting a Beatle reunion when all four played on one of his smash albums. His acting roles, studio sessions, and vastly entertaining albums keep him in the public eye.

ways to get ahead.

The film opened in Los Angeles in October 1974. It was announced that Ringo would be there in person, so I bought my ticket and hoped. They wouldn't let us into the theater until the "stars" had arrived, so I was stuck behind a crowd of what must have been the tallest freaks in the world. Ringo's car drove up and he got out while a few squeals rose from the distaff side. Finally we were allowed in. I had brought the *Ringo* album with me on the off chance he might sign autographs.

Ringo sat a few rows from the back; I glanced quickly at him over my shoulder, not wanting to stare, as I took a seat near the front. The theater was dark; Ringo wore his insect-like sunglasses and a heavy beard, as if he weren't there at all. It dawned on me that there would probably be no introduction of Ringo by an MC, or any chance to talk to him unless I took the initiative. I boldly went to his row and waited until he'd finished chatting with a girl behind him before I spoke. Ringo had on a button advertising John's *Walls and Bridges* album and was sitting next to Harry Nilsson, who glowered at me when I stepped forward to catch Ringo's attention.

"Ringo?"

"Yes?" he said, turning to me.

I swallowed. "Hi. I just wanted to say you've been a friend for a lot of years."

"Have I?" he asked.

"And I wanted to thank you for it," I burbled, handing him the album. "Would you mind . . ."

"Oh, well, if you buy the album I'll have to sign, won't I?" he said. He took the record and drew his name on the inside sleeve with a flourish. As he handed

it back, my hand accidentally brushed his . . . and there, in the strange half-light of the theater, like it was a waking dream, I realized I had made contact with the hands that had drummed on "I Want to Hold Your Hand," that had given "Hey Jude" its drive. I had encountered a legend that had shaped the world and changed my life.

"When I'm ninety-five," Ringo said to an interviewer, "and it's This Is Your Life time, they'll still be referring to me as 'ex-Beatle.' None of us is ever going to lose that association. Sometimes we would like to, but then again it does have its advantages. It's still the best way I know to get a good table at a restaurant."

There's another benefit, Ringo. You have friends wherever you go.

And so it went. The Beatle image won't die, not for a long time. Even while the group was calling it quits, four albums (*Hey Jude, In the Beginning,* and two album sets, *The Beatles 1962-1970*) were released. A novelty record called *The Masked Marauders,* which supposedly featured John, Paul, and George in a jam session with Mick Jagger and Bob Dylan, caused quite a stir. Beatles trading fairs and film festivals are increasingly commonplace; Capitol Records sponsors a Beatles swap meet the first Sunday of every month. Bootleg albums and tapes, some carrying genuine collector's items like the Christmas Messages, some carrying false Beatle pieces like "L. S. Bumblebee," flourish. "Beatle days" are still promoted on radio stations (one even gave away a twenty-three-foot-statue of Ringo as a prize), although Beatles oldies don't do very well anymore in "vote for your favorite" contests. A promoter offered the Beatles $50,000,000 for a live, closed-circuit TV concert. And I'm still waiting for somebody to get smart enough to release the album of the Beatles 1964 concert at the Hollywood Bowl, the recording of the Beatles live in Hamburg, and the two-record set of oldies from *Let It Be* sessions, called *Look Back.* Capitol has promised them; let's all hope.

But for now I'll have to be content with the fact that there are four people releasing records of high-quality music instead of one group doing one album a year. In their solo years the four Beatles have already produced twice the number of original songs they had in all their years as Beatles. John, in his music, looks behind him to his past; Paul looks ahead; George looks up; and Ringo looks—well, Ringo looks mournful.

The Beatles, literally by themselves, overthrew all that came before and set in motion all that will come after. They infused their decade with youth and energy and communicated it to millions. And they communicated it to me. The time came to replace them with the artistic encapsulation of the experience of maturity found at Woodstock, in the bloodbath of Vietnam, and in the abrasion of Watergate. The time came, the Beatles rightfully relinquished the crown and went their separate ways, but no one took it up again. That very fact establishes their superiority. No one has been able to, no one has dared to, move in and fill the void. The dream is not over, it will never be over, until another dream can take its place.

Beatles 4-Ever!

1976

Looking forward . . . looking back . . .

To call the recent explosion of enthusiasm about the Beatles a "revival" is like referring to the Renaissance as a shopping-center parking-lot arts-and-crafts display. Sparked by American rock promoter Bill Sargent's offer of fifty million dollars for a one-shot closed-circuit broadcast of a reunion concert, rumors of a Beatle get-together, prevalent since the day they broke

(Above) The Beatles. On the next pages are photographs to remind us of the time that has passed. . . . and of how short that time has seemed.

up, began taking on greater significance. George Harrison's father told a reporter for the London *Daily Mirror* that his son had said "he and the other lads will be getting together for a show." When informed of his father's comment, George was surprised but stated that if the others wanted a reunion, he would go along with it. Although none of the Beatles even acknowledged Sargent's offer, a spokesman for McCartney said, "If the former Beatles do meet up with one another again, it would be no surprise. They tend to turn up at one another's concerts. They are all friends despite their old disputes." But McCartney himself responded by saying that a reunion just for the money "would ruin the whole Beatle thing for me. The only way the Beatles could come back together again would be if we wanted to do something musically."

Meanwhile, on both sides of the Atlantic, Beatle excitement swelled. In England all twenty-three of the Beatles' singles, including the never-released single of "Yesterday," were reissued in a special collector's series. Each record placed in the British Top 100; "Yesterday," "Hey Jude," "Paperback Writer," and "Get Back" were all in the top thirty, despite protests from other record companies who felt only new songs should be represented in the charts. EMI marketing director Bob Mercer attributes the resurgence of Beatlemania to the fact that a new generation has grown up, one that missed the Beatles' "golden era."

In America, Capitol Records, never one to lag behind when it comes to promotional ballyhoo, followed the English lead with a Beatles Blitz of reissued singles and albums, spearheaded by the new/old anthology package *Rock 'n' Roll Music.* The two-record set, consisting of fast-paced, heavily electric selections from former albums, offers only one real advantage to Beatles collectors—the first album appearance of "Slow Down." The outside cover is an amusing drawing of the Beatles, but the inside is an atrocious mishmash of Coke glasses, a jukebox, and Marilyn Monroe on a drive-in movie screen. Ridiculous—the Beatles were the *Sixties,* not the Fifties. Considering what might have been released instead, *Rock 'n' Roll Music* is a disappointment. Why

rehash the old chestnuts when so much previously unreleased material lies moldering in the Capitol vaults? Why not at least preserve a few more "unalbumized" B sides? Oh well. Call it a gesture and let it go at that.

Capitol flooded record stores with posters and mobiles and supplied select outlets with a documentary/animated film of Beatle clips and photos. A Cleveland store dropped a six-foot model of the Yellow Submarine in the middle of their display floor. Radio stations sponsored contests. Said a friend, "The only thing missing is the Beatles themselves."

Hard on the heels of the Beatles bonanza came McCartney in his first tour of America. His album, *At the Speed of Sound*, released to coincide with the tour, is a well-meaning attempt to spotlight the other members of the band, who, with the exception of Linda, hold their own fairly well against Paul's towering talent.

At first I couldn't stand "Silly Love Songs," but its catchy little rhythm and bouncy string and trumpet section eventually worked their magic on me. "Let 'Em In" is fun, but "Cook of the House" is an awful bore. "Beware My Love" really churns along, proving Paul more of a rocker than he is usually given credit for being. "Time to Hide" and "Must Do Something About It" are beautifully melodic and give Denny Laine and Joe English a chance to show their vocal abilities.

Wings' tour was delayed when Jimmy McCulloch slipped in the bathroom of a Paris hotel and fractured a finger on his left hand, but it was rescheduled for a month later. Wings opened in Fort Worth, Texas, on May 3 to a cheering, enthusiastic crowd. Paul brought his group to Kansas City on May 29, a playdate not on the original schedule, and the entire Midwest caught what one radio station described as "McCartney fever."

The Beatles passed from noisy, unmanageable dockside scruffs in Liverpool to an energetic, charismatic group of Hamburg toughs with Stu Sutcliff (opposite and left) to an irresistible force of talent, enthusiasm, and artistry.

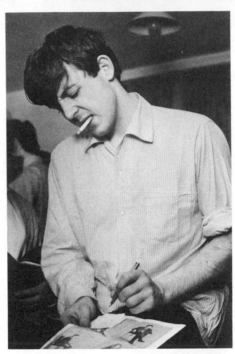

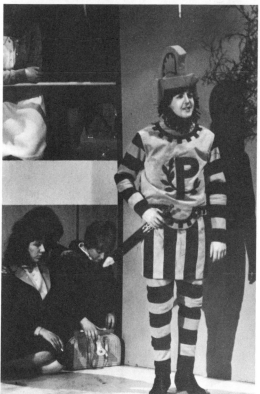

The Beatles succeeded because they never took themselves seriously; they gave themselves to the world, entertained us, made us laugh and made us cry. They tolerated the crowds of photographers and silly costumes (including those for a parody of Pyramus and Thisbe, above) with patience and self-effacement. They were rewarded with record honors, the undying adoration of millions of fans around the world, and a permanent niche in the happy islands of our subconscious.

The concert triumphantly met and exceeded expectations. Unlike George, who poutingly refused to cater to the fans, Paul included authentic versions of Beatles songs, saluting the past but never allowing it to dominate.

I thought it a little insulting that Linda and the other Wings sang the backup vocals on "Lady Madonna" because I felt that was territory only the Beatles should have trod. But Paul's touchingly simply solo rendition of "Yesterday" more than adequately compensated. I

158

The Beatles' greatest gift to the world was their music; they somehow managed to strike a chord on their guitars that reverberated across barriers of age, race, and distance. Their songs absorbed the emotions of an era, distilled them into a wine that was alternately heady and delicate, a wine of happiness, joyousness, and hope. It may never happen again; I'm glad it happened once. John, Paul, George, Ringo: to themselves, Beatles once; to those who love them, Beatles forever!

was strangely moved, as I have never been before, by "The Long and Winding Road," which rang out with clarity unhampered by strings or choirs. Actually, the concert succeeded most when Wings as a band performed its own materials. The show sparked with visual effect such as bubbles, smoke, flash pots, and a dazzling, dancing laser beam, but it was the music—and McCartney—that was the star.

Paul's efforts to associate himself completely with his new band have succeeded. I was a little saddened when I first heard about the tour, because I turned to a friend and exclaimed, "McCartney's coming to Kansas City!"

"Oh," she said, "you mean Wings?"
I hesitated. "Yeah, I guess I do mean Wings."

Paul is no longer the "ex-Beatle"; I guess the same can be said of the other three. They have each established themselves as individuals, with unique abilities and distinguished talents. The criticism has been voiced that a Beatles reunion would result in a giant clash of egos, that irresistible forces would collide with immovable objects. In Paul's words, "It would be like reheating a soufflé."

Perhaps. But then, perhaps not. I believe that a reunion would produce more than just a passing breeze of nostalgia. The Beatles are six years older and six years wiser; apart from one another they have learned where their strengths and weaknesses lie. They have had a chance to step back and look at the Beatles as an entity in itself. I think now they could reassume the group structure, bringing to it fresh ideas and new momentum, avoiding past missteps and the staleness that had begun to creep into their music. The fusion of such great chunks of talent could result in a joyous explosion of music, mania, and magic.

Perhaps not. But perhaps.

Acknowledgments

This book is a valentine to the Beatles and to the other friends who shared the experience with me. It could not have been written without the love and help offered by all members of my family, especially my dear dear mother and father, and Lisa Doermann, Kathy Atkinson, Margie Benson, Corky Carrel, Laurie Chipman, Gary Christian, Rick Enlow, Bob Evans, Diana Foster, Susan Hazen, Esther Hope, Paul Gentine, Debbie Jacquez, Sue Lyons, Vickie C. Marlatt, David Parrish, Herb Rook, Pat Schaefer, Suzi Shea, Tom Smith, Mike Sturley, Sue and the Wings Fun Club, Melinda Unsworth, Pat Vilas, Mary Lee Wilson, Mark Winkler, Don Young, and Apple Records.

I am indebted to Dezo Hoffman for his help and cooperation in supplying a large proportion of the photographs in this book. Also to the following for their contributions: Stephen Goldblatt, John Kelly, Bob Gruen, Rex Features, Galaxy International, Camera Press, SKR Photos, Syndication International, Hipgnosis, Linda McCartney, Johnny Rozsa, Tony Brainsby, Robert Ellis, Capitol Records, R.C.A. Records, A & M Records, Brian Southall, E.M.I. Records, Roger Watt, Mick Rock, Mike Nicholson, Don of Acme Attractions, Kimi O'Brien, Michael Gross, *The Los Angeles Times*. TAL Enterprises, and Bob Evans for the back cover photograph of me.

The lines from "The Fat Budgie," on page 129, from *A Spaniard in the Works* by John Lennon, are reprinted by kind permission of the publishers, Jonathan Cape Ltd., London.

My gratitude to Sheila Rock for her painstaking and thorough work in researching the pictures for the book, and to Steve Ridgeway and Julie Harris for their beautiful layout and cover designs.

My appreciation to the Pyramid People—Carol Plaine, Norman Goldfind, Marilyn Houston, Mike Winn, Mary Traina, John Rutledge, and Ron Adelson—for their patience, hard work, and encouragement.

My thanks and love to Jeannie Sakol and Stephanie Bennett of Delilah Books, without whose faith and efforts this book would not have been.

Special thanks to Peter Marston for his generosity and his invaluable contribution.